Meet It With Faith

Meet It With Faith

Martha Smock

UNITY® Books

Unity Village, MO 64065

Revised paperback edition 1995

Eleven printings through 1982

To receive a catalog of all Unity publications (books, cassettes, and
magazines) or to place an order, call the Customer Service Department: 1-800-669-0282 or (816) 251-3580.

Cover art and design by Jackie Prosser

 The New Revised Standard Version is used for
all Bible verses unless otherwise noted.

LIBRARY OF CONGRESS CATALOGING-IN-PUBLICATION DATA

Smock, Martha.
    Meet It With Faith / Martha Smock. — Rev. pbk. ed.
        p. cm.
    1. Spiritual life—Unity School of Christianity.   2. Unity School
of Christianity—Doctrines.   I. Title.
BX9890.U505S66   1995
248.4'8997—dc20   94-35169
ISBN 0-87159-074-3 (alk. paper)   : $9.95
Canada GST R132529033

Unity Books feels a sacred trust to be a healing presence in
the world. By printing with biodegradable soybean ink on
recycled paper, we believe we are doing our part to be wise
stewards of our Earth's resources.

c.3

Table of Contents

Part I

You Can Be Calm, Relaxed, Trusting

Chapter 1

Let

When the Bible describes God's creation of the world, the word it uses is *let*. "Let there be a firmament .... Let the waters under the heaven be gathered together unto one place .... Let the earth bring forth grass .... Let there be lights in the firmament of the heaven .... Let the waters bring forth abundantly the moving creature ... and fowl that may fly above the earth .... Let the earth bring forth the living creature after his kind .... Let us make man in our image, after our likeness" (Gen. 1:6-26 KJV).

We, in creating our individual world, sometimes do not use the word *let*; rather, we scheme, we plan, we strive to attain our ends. We feel that we have to fight to attain some desired good, and then we believe that we have to fight to keep it.

All we ever have to do is let goodness in. Where we have stormed and pounded on the gates of heaven, now we learn that heaven is within us and the door opens inward. It opens easily and smoothly to our word *let*.

To let God take over in our lives is to be set free from willfulness and fretting. It is to be set free from dependence on our human powers alone. It is to let ourselves be God-inspired, God-filled, and God-directed.

Life is really a process of "letting go and letting." This is the divine rhythm, the expiration and the inspiration of the Holy Spirit.

We need continually to let go of any negative beliefs, any destructive emotions, any tendency to resist change; and we need continually to let—to let the Spirit of God take over in us, to fill us with new life, to re-create us in mind, body, and Spirit.

We may well ask ourselves, "What am I holding on to?" Sometimes we are holding on to a way of life that is no longer possible to us, a way of life that we have outgrown. But we resist change, we do not want to see the infringement of new ways, new ideas. At this point, we need to consciously let go, to declare our willingness to let go and let God and to declare our complete faith and trust in God, which we have been denying by our fear of change, our fear that something will interfere with that to which we have become accustomed. Let us turn to God in complete trust. Let us surrender ourselves, commit ourselves to God's love and infinite goodness. Let us say: "Father, I let go of fear, I let go of all that has limited me or bound me. I let go of my personal will, my self-pride, my determination to do things my own way. I let go of self and let Your Spirit take over in me." *Let* becomes a creative word for us as we say in faith and without fear: "Let there be light in my mind; let there be light in my life."

Every day of our lives we are making decisions, and we are choosing the kind of life that is to be ours. The total character of our thoughts and attitudes determines how much or how little of Spirit we are letting into our lives.

If we need guidance in some situation, what do we do, where do we turn? Sometimes we do not take our need for guidance to God. We handle everything on a surface level, and even if we make a good decision, we often worry and fret over what the outcome is to be. When we form the habit of taking all of our needs to God first in prayer, we find that we are filled with a sense of rightness and direction that we can gain in no other way. We are filled with a feeling of freedom and peace when we pray about all matters; and even though the answer may not be yet apparent, we are able to go about our lives with a calm and confident spirit, sure of God's presence, sure of the right outworking of every situation.

In our thoughts, in our prayers, let us follow this pattern of letting go and letting. *I let go of all belief in negation. I let the Spirit of God fill me, move through me, renew me, mind, soul, and body.*

In any healing need, this same principle of letting go and letting may be applied with sure results. Healing comes as we let go of all belief in disease, as we let go of tension or anxiety, as we let go of fear. Healing comes as we let the life of God find free and full access through us, as we have faith in the mighty healing power within us, and as we let the healing life of God fill us and thrill us from the tops of our heads to the soles of our feet.

If we find ourselves in a situation that is inharmonious or if we are disturbed and upset by what someone else has said or done to hurt us or cause us to suffer unjustly, we need first of all to let go, to deliberately let go of all belief in the power of anyone to hurt us or make us unhappy, to let go of any belief in injustice or suffering. And in letting go we open the way for an inrush of God's healing, transforming love. We let God take over in us, in the situation, in everyone concerned; and in letting go and letting God we find peace and joy of Spirit.

We are meant for joyous, happy, healthy living. We were created in God's image and after His likeness. Let us remember this. Let us let God take over in us, fill us, inspire us, renew us. Let us let God's creative Spirit transform us into new and living souls.

Chapter 2

Be Still, and Know

When things do not seem to work out in the way we had hoped or planned, we may be tempted to give way to feelings of discouragement or frustration. But if we have faith in the Truth that God is at work in and through all things, if we hold to the belief that all things are in God's care and that divine order prevails, we are able to hold steady. We are able to remain calm and poised. We are able to be patient in the face of delays or apparent obstacles.

From our present viewpoint it may seem that there is only one way for our good to come forth in a particular situation; but from the overall viewpoint, from the viewpoint of Truth, there are no limitations—there are endless possibilities for the emergence of good.

The thing that we need to remember is that there is only God. If we say this to ourselves and live with this thought, "There is only God," we are kept from anxiety, we are free from fear, and we live in an atmosphere of faith and assurance. There is only God; there is only one presence and one power, the

7

presence and power of good. There is only God, so there is only good.

God is the one activity at work in us and in our lives, and this activity always produces good results. Where God is there is life, there is power, there is peace; where God is there is fulfillment.

Where is God? God is where we are. We live and move and have our being in the divine Presence. So even when we cannot see our way, even when we cannot see how things can possibly work out, we need only know that God is with us. Where we are God is, and where God is there is the perfect answer to every need.

Many persons think of God as a last resort. If things get bad enough they fall on their knees in prayer, hoping for a miracle to save them. God is—first, last, and always. The more we can learn to live daily, momently in the Presence, the more we can learn to keep our thoughts God-centered, the freer we are of fear and the less need we have for miracles.

One of the most helpful verses in the Bible is found in the 46th Psalm: "Be still, and know that I am God!" When you do not know where to turn or what to do to find your way out of some difficulty, take these words to yourself: "Be still, and know that I am God!" As you say them to your mind, to your emotions, to your thoughts, to your body, you will make way for God to enter into your consciousness. You will cease trying to tell God what you need, you will not try to tell God what to do; rather you will be still and listen. You will give God a chance to express through you, to be known to you, and to open the way before you.

Many times our greatest need is for stillness. We scatter our energy and our forces by talking about ourselves or our problems. The true silence that is communion with God is more than just being still. The beginning has to be a simple act of stopping all the outer talk, the outer striving and straining—the basic act of being still.

"Be still"—this is the first step. "And know that I am God"—this is the second. When we are still and know that there is only God—that the Presence infolds us, surrounds us, and fills us with power, with life, with substance—when we know that we are one with God, then we see that there are really no problems. There is only God, and in God is all that we can ever need or desire.

What is your need? Is it healing? Is it guidance in making some decision? Is it supply? Is it a job? Is it freedom from confusion and inharmony in your environment? Your answer is with you now. "Be still, and know that I am God. I am life, I am health, I am wisdom, I am guidance, I am supply, I am fulfillment, I am peace, I am the perfection you seek. I am God. I am with you now."

Chapter 3

You Can Be Calm, Relaxed, Trusting

When we feel tense, nervous, or keyed up and someone tells us to relax, we may lash out in resentment. Of course we would like to relax, we think to ourselves, but how can we, the way we feel!

To say to ourselves, "You must relax," does not help. Usually saying it makes us feel more tense, if anything. The reason for our tension and anxiety may actually be bound up in these two words, "You must." We keep saying them to ourselves over and over. "You must finish all that work." "You must hurry." "You must make a decision." We may have put ourselves under such continual pressure that what we need more than anything else is to quit telling ourselves what we must do. We need to find a different approach to things so that we do not keep building up tension.

Can we learn to relax and gain control of our nerves, our reactions, our emotions? Yes, but (paradoxically) not by trying to relax but by not trying to!

Anyone who has suffered with insomnia knows that the more he tries to go to sleep, the more he thinks about sleep, the more wide-awake he becomes.

If we are not to try to relax, what are we to do? How are we to find release from taut nerves, keyed-up emotions, or anxious feelings? When the disciples were in the boat with Jesus and the storm arose, they awakened Him and cried, "Teacher, do you not care that we are perishing?" (Mk. 4:38) And Jesus spoke to the wind and the waves, "Peace! Be still!" (Mk. 4:39) We have the Mind of Christ in us, and like the disciples who awakened the sleeping Christ, we need to wake up and rouse the Christ Mind in us. It is this Mind in us that speaks the word of peace in us and through us and calms the inner storms and stresses. "The mind of the Spirit is life and peace" (Rom. 8:6 ASV).

When we have things to meet that seem difficult or trying, let us say to ourselves: *The Mind of Spirit is in me and the Mind of Spirit is life and peace.* We do not function on our own power alone. We are linked with God, we have within us the one Power, the one Presence, the one Mind. What we cannot do, God in us can do. What seems impossible to us is possible with God.

The surest way to overcome tension, stress, and strain is to rely on the power of God in us, which is greater than our fear and which works powerfully in and through us. Our minds need not be places of confusion but places of peace, of confidence, and of quietness and trust, for our minds are one with the Mind of God. We have the Mind of Spirit.

To know that we have the Mind of Spirit, to let this

Mind function through us is to change our whole lives and thoughts. Where before we have worried and fretted over our health, our finances, our families, and our futures, we now begin to look at things differently. We see that we can relax; we can let go because God is in charge. What we cannot do of our own selves God can do through us; what we cannot do for our dear ones God can do through them.

To know that we have the Mind of Spirit and that we are one with the creative Source gives us an inner confidence and assurance. We are able to approach everything in our lives easily, happily, and successfully.

The storms may come, but we hear the indwelling Christ speaking the word of peace through us. We need to take time every day to be still and meditate on the life-giving, peace-giving Presence within us, to open our minds and hearts to the light of Spirit, the peace of Spirit, the joy of Spirit. We shall find that there is a difference in our prayers, too, when we pray in the realization that we are part of the great creative power of the universe and that in us and through us flows the power of God. Our prayers will no longer be pleadings but clear and joyful awakenings.

We find, too, that as we become consciously aware of the Mind of Spirit in us, the Mind that is life and peace, our feelings and attitudes toward ourselves and others change. When other persons have the power to make us bitter or resentful, we do not really understand and know ourselves as spiritual beings. We are on the defensive and on guard; we are easily hurt because we undervalue or underrate ourselves. When we know ourselves spiritually, we also begin to know others spiritually. We see them as we see ourselves, as children of God, and we find it easier to love, to forgive, and to understand. A sure way to peace of mind and freedom from tension is to have a loving, forgiving spirit, to let go of the past hurts, and to remember no more the thing that was said or done that brought unhappiness.

The Mind of Spirit in us is always standing at a point of newness, of beginning. Through this Mind we are made new. "Be transformed by the renewing of your minds" (Rom. 12:2). Through this Mind we are kept in quietness and confidence. By this Mind we are healed, mentally, physically, and emotionally.

Chapter 4

Flow Along With Your Good; Grow Along With Your Good

If you have any feeling of stress or strain about anything in your life—your home, your work, your family, your health, your finances—take this thought and rest in it, relax in it: *I flow along with my good; I grow along with my good.*

Most of our problems arise from our trying too hard to work things out or from trying to make persons and situations conform to our ideas of how things should be. How quickly problems are dissolved once we are able to let go of them and trust God to work in and through us to bring about good!

Many times we set up resistance in ourselves; we do not like the idea of change, we want to keep things as they are, and yet something in us is not satisfied. We want our lives to be richer and fuller.

When you say to yourself, *I flow along with my good;*

I grow along with my good, think of yourself as wholly receptive to all of God's blessings, as completely non-resistant to your good, as welcoming new ideas, new ways, new life. To flow along with your good is to feel yourself a part of the living stream of God and to know that effortlessly and easily you go from good to good. You are sustained and upheld by the current of divine love and power.

You grow along with your good as you think of yourself as a child of God, learning and growing every moment of your life. You live in a climate of growth as you live in the presence of God and feel yourself surrounded and enfolded by the unchanging good of God.

If you are tempted to get tense or anxious, remind yourself: *God is with me, God is at work, God is all good, and I trust God to bless me and all that concerns me.*

You may get discouraged at times, for it may seem that you have not come very far on the path of understanding. Just when you think you have learned to really trust God, something happens to shake your faith and make you question your ability to cope successfully with the affairs of your life. But never fear: you are learning, you are growing, and you have much more faith and understanding than you realize you have. You are on the path of light; and even when you cannot see the way, God is opening up the way before you and is shedding more and more light into your mind.

A child grows without realizing it, and so do we. We may not realize how far we have come, but God rejoices in our progress and Spirit in us continually calls us forward. A child does not anxiously watch her growth and unfoldment, and neither do we need to watch ours. We only need to let ourselves grow and unfold naturally and joyously.

There are some who seem to resist everything. Their first reaction to any suggestion is a negative one; their first response to any challenge is "I can't." If we know anyone like this we can bless that person with this idea: *You flow along with your good; you grow along with your good.* Even the person who seems to have built up walls of resistance has a spirit in the innermost Self that is receptive and responsive to prayer and longs to be free, happy, and in tune with God and humankind, in tune with his or her own good.

The joyous thing about flowing along with our good is that there are so many happy surprises along the way. Even if we were given some magic power that would enable us to sit down and plan our lives so they would include everything we ever wanted or dreamed of, still our imaginations could not conceive of the delightful and unexpected turns that life can take and of the forms in which our good can come to us. We need not and should not outline how our good is to come or limit ourselves by praying too specifically. We need only to grow in our faith and understanding; to know that God's good plans and purposes are unfolding in us and through us, that our good comes to us under divine law.

During the times when we seem to be standing still or even going backward, let us not lose heart. Then, more than ever, our need is to let God do perfect work and to trust God to bless, to heal, to prosper, and to make all things right.

Chapter 5

God Is in the Midst of You

God is in the midst of you. This is a wonderful Truth to know.

Do you need healing? God is in the midst of you as life. God's life is the only life, and this is the life that fills your body; that flows in and through every part of you.

There is no condition that is beyond God's power to heal; there is no disease that is resistant to God's healing life.

Hold to this idea of life, expand your faith in it, and think of it as filling you through and through. Rejoice and give thanks that God is in the midst of you as life—healing, strengthening, renewing life.

If ever you feel alone, separated from family or friends, or thrown upon your own resources, stop, think, remember, and rejoice that you are not alone and that God is in the midst of you as your Guide, your Comforter, your constant Companion. God is with you, and with God, in God, you can do and be all things.

Wherever you are, you are in the presence of God and God is with you—mighty and unfailing in the midst of you. Just to know this, just to say to yourself, "God is with me," gives you renewed strength and courage and inspires in you the will to go on, the perseverance to conquer loneliness and fear.

God is in the midst of you right now, right where you stand.

At those times when your way seems dark before you, when you do not know which way to turn, God is in the midst of you as light. You need only to turn inward to become immediately aware of God's guiding presence.

> "And the crooked shall be made straight,
>   and the rough places plain."
>   —Isaiah 40:4 KJV

You do not need to see the whole way before you; you need only to trust the Spirit of God in the midst of you to direct you step by step into the way of your highest good. The darkness lifts as you look to God in the midst of you. Your doubts and questionings disappear as you open your mind and heart to light.

You may have thought that you had to depend on the wisdom of others, that you had to wait for someone else to show you the way before you could proceed, but you have your own light, the light of God in the midst of you. Follow this inward light and you cannot fail to find your way. Walking in the light of God's presence, you find your way out of every difficulty, and you emerge stronger and wiser from every experience.

God is in the midst of you as love. If you have longed for more love and happiness in your life, or if you have wished that you could be closer and more important to others, it may be that you feel as you do because God's Spirit in you is seeking greater expression. God in the midst of you is love, divine love, and this love needs to be expressed, to be given forth. Let your prayer be; "Father, teach me to love. Let me show forth Your love in kindness, in generosity, in consideration, in forgiveness, and in understanding. Let me learn to see others as Your children. Let me learn to love all people as You love them."

"I have loved you with an everlasting love; therefore I have continued my faithfulness to you" (Jer. 31:3). God is in the midst of you as a great outpouring of love. You are beloved of God, needed by God, important to God. Just as God needs you as a channel through which love is expressed, so also God needs you as a recipient of divine love. God's faithfulness is brought into expression in you and for you; it is shared with the world through you and by you. God in the midst of you is love. God's divine love is the law of your life, the law of your being.

God is in the midst of you. What does this mean? It means that God is at the heart of your being. God is the secret core of your life. God is in the thoughts you think. God is the motivating power behind your acts. To know that God is with you, to know that God is in the midst of you, to know that in God you live and move and have your being, is to live in faith, to draw every breath as an act of faith, and to speak every word as an affirmation of faith.

God is in the midst of you. Know this, carry this knowledge with you, and remind yourself of it many times throughout every day. God is in the midst of you, your all in all, the perfect fulfillment of every need.

Chapter 6

Let Not Your Heart Be Troubled

God can help and can heal any condition or situation, no matter how frightening or distressing the appearances. "Peace I leave with you; my peace I give to you. I do not give to you as the world gives. Do not let your hearts be troubled, and do not let them be afraid" (Jn.14:27). "I am with you always" (Mt. 28:20).

If you are concerned or disturbed about something, say these words of Jesus over to yourself. Say them and listen to them. Think of the living, loving Christ speaking them to you, through you.

Let not your heart be troubled by sickness. Christ is within you as healing life. There is nothing to fear, for with God all things are possible; with God there are no incurable conditions. Christ is saying to you now, "You have been made well!" (Jn. 5:14)

Let not your heart be troubled by injustice or unfair treatment. Give everything over to the loving

Christ and know that this Spirit is able to make all things right. Hold fast to your faith in God, to your faith in the good, and keep your heart and mind open to the forgiving, loving benediction of the Christ. You are beloved of God; you are one with Christ. You are surrounded and enfolded by perfect peace that the world cannot give, the peace that is God's gift to your heart, mind, and life.

Let not your heart be troubled, neither let it be fearful if there seems to be lack in your life. There is no reason to fear that you will not have supply to meet present or future needs, for your supply comes to you from God and you are always one with your source. Have faith in God and pray for greater faith. As you are open and receptive and responsive to the Father's guidance, ways will open to you, new avenues of supply will be revealed, and a way out of lack and limitation will be clearly shown to you.

Let not your heart be troubled if gossip comes to your ears that is cruel and upsetting. Make this an opportunity to bless everyone concerned and to pray for light to be shed into every mind, for love and forgiveness to rule in every heart, and for understanding and tolerance to replace suspicion and condemnation. You can easily and quickly dismiss negative gossip from your own mind so that it is remembered no more, and you can help to erase it and its effects through giving it over to the forgiving Christ.

Let not your heart be troubled by the problems and needs of your dear ones. Even when it seems that there is nothing you can do, that you must stand by and see a dear one suffer, do not forget that God is with your dear one, that God's love is greater than any human love.

Have faith in the Spirit of God in your dear one, have faith in God to guide, to bless, to heal, and to help. You are not to stand by with a troubled heart, but with a heart of faith, a heart that is filled with love, a heart that rejoices in the power of God at work.

"Peace I leave with you; my peace I give to you. I do not give to you as the world gives. Do not let your hearts be troubled, and do not let them be afraid." "I am with you always."

When you pick up your newspaper and read disquieting, fearful things about the world situation, let these words of Jesus take away all fear. The peace of Jesus Christ is here now, in our minds and hearts and in the minds and hearts of people all over the world. The Spirit of justice, the Spirit of Truth, the Spirit of freedom, the Spirit of unity is abroad. The peace of Christ is present with us. The Christ power is working now to remake the earth.

> "For I am about to create new heavens
>   and a new earth;
>   the former things shall not be
>   remembered
>   or come to mind."
>   —Isaiah 65:17

Part II

How Important Is It?

Chapter 7

The Unusual Reaction

Most persons are not surprised at usual reactions; it is the unusual reaction that often astonishes.

Two persons meet similar problems; one goes down under the problem, the other rises above it and transforms the whole experience into something good.

When we face anything in our lives in a spirit of faith and trust, we may be sure that our reactions will not be considered the usual ones. To look beyond appearances to the underlying, undeviating presence and power of God is to rise above anxiety or fear. To know with a sure and abiding knowing that God is with us, that we are forever one with God and God's good, is to rise above any feeling of discouragement or any thought of giving up in defeat or despair.

If we seem to be in financial need, if our incomes do not stretch far enough to cover necessities, we would not be considered unusual if we reacted fearfully or if we became anxious or tense in wondering how our needs were to be met, where the money was to come from, or where to turn for help.

But when we rely on God, we bypass the usual reactions and we rise above them quickly. We take our stand for Truth, affirm it, believe it, stay with it. We are strong and unshaken because we know our oneness with God and because we know that Spirit is our unfailing, all-providing Source. We know as Jesus knew that "your heavenly Father knows that you need all these things" (Mt. 6:32); that "all these things will be given to you" (Mt. 6:33) as we seek and find the kingdom of God within us, the secret place where we are one with God and with our good.

If we are burdened with responsibilities or cares, if it seems that more is piled upon our shoulders than we are able to bear, no one would be surprised to hear us say: "I just cannot go on. Things have become too hard for me. I shall never be able to do all that is before me to do."

But when we search for something beyond the usual reaction we find it as we pray; we find it as we remember the promises of the Bible. We transform thoughts of weakness into strength through identifying ourselves with God and through knowing as Jesus knew that we of ourselves can do nothing, but that we can do and be all things through our oneness with the Father.

The usual reaction from those who are alone, who are without family or friends, who seem to have nothing to give them joy or brightness, is that of sadness and despair. They feel forgotten, unloved, unwanted. But the one who trusts God says: "I am not alone. I am one with the love of God. I am one with all others through the living unity of Spirit." We may take what seems an unusual stand in the face of the conditions of our lives, but such a stand renews us in Spirit, lifts our hearts, fills us with the love of God that is like a magnet to attract our good to us.

When we are filled with a feeling of God's love and let it find expression through us, we cannot help but draw into our circle those who need what we have to give, those who are able to give what we need.

When we feel bound or trapped by life and circumstances, our usual reaction is to blame someone else, to feel sorry for ourselves, or to believe that we have not had the opportunities that others have had. Herein is where we need to take a transcendent view of ourselves and our lives, to look at ourselves as children of light, as spiritual beings, to know that in Spirit, in God, we are unfettered and unbound, triumphant, glorious, splendid, and free!

To lift our thoughts above self to Spirit is to find Truth, Truth that sets us free with the only freedom that matters, the freedom of Spirit. When we have this freedom, we have everything. Nothing can bind us or limit us or keep us from our good. Nothing can stand between us and God. Knowing this, we are free.

Every time we pray in faith and understanding, every time we affirm Truth in the face of appearances to the contrary, we are transcending the old self, the usual reactions; we are making an unusual reaction, the kind that seems to defy explanation, the kind that rests and relies solely on faith in God.

Unusual results in response to prayer we call miracles. The miracle-working power is present in us always, for what we think of as a miracle is, in God's sight, the right and natural outworking of the law of good that rules our lives.

You can work with your reactions and your attitudes so that they do not follow the same old lines. You are capable of the unusual reaction, for you have the Spirit of God in you to inspire you. You have the love of God in you to make you strong. You have the light of God in you to transform and make bright with glory the thoughts of your mind and the days of your life.

How can you do anything but react with faith, with courage, with power when you know that you are part of God's good? All that you need or ever will need flows to you and through you—unimpeded, marked, as it were, with your name—your own from God!

Chapter 8

Two Words to Remember

There are some key ideas that have a great deal of power. Just to think of them sets the law of good into motion.

Divine order is such an idea. Perhaps this is an idea that you work with effectively. Perhaps it is one that you need to give more thought to or that you need to actively use. Just the two words *divine order* are a blessing in themselves. They are an affirmation of faith, a declaration that God is in charge, that God is at work. If you find that you do not easily remember long affirmations of Truth, here are two words that you can easily remember, two words that can work wonders for you—*divine order*.

When things go wrong on those days you feel as though you got up on the wrong side of the bed, how needed is this idea of divine order! Before you let yourself sigh and exclaim, "It's just one of those days when everything seems to go wrong," stop right there and silently, firmly, faithfully affirm: *Divine order*. Give thanks that divine order is established in you, in all that you do, in the work of your hands, in your home, and in your family. The trend of your thinking and feeling will be changed by the idea of divine order, and your day will be one to remember and bless.

When you work in the realization that you are under God's law of love, the law of Good, that divine order is established in and for you, you find yourself functioning on a new level. Your mind is clearer, your body is stronger, and your emotions are calm and unperturbed. You are able to meet everything with ease and to accomplish all things successfully.

If you are getting ready for a trip or making vacation plans, it is most helpful to affirm divine order. You will not find yourself getting tense, tired, or anxious about details as you affirm divine order every step of the way. Keep knowing as you make your plans and arrangements that divine order is established. Affirm as you travel, as you meet new and different experiences: *Divine order is established in all my comings and goings. Divine order makes my way easy, happy, and uncomplicated.* Even so-called inanimate objects respond to this idea of divine order. The car that is blessed with the thought of divine order will perform much more smoothly. Try it for yourself and see.

If in your home or place of business you find yourself confronted with unfinished work that looms up depressingly before you, declare divine order instead of looking at it and thinking that you will never get it done. Know that you are given the strength you need to accomplish what is before you. When you work in the knowledge that God is with you, that through God you can do all things, you are working in the spirit of divine order and you do not find things difficult. Everything seems to flow along. Divine order is the easy way, the way of light.

When you stay with this idea of divine order, you see that it carries you through all kinds of situations. Anyone who holds firmly to faith in divine order can prove the power of God, can bring forth right and good answers where no solution seems possible. God is love, God is all good, God is justice.

If it seems to you that you are being unjustly treated, that some person or situation is depriving you of what belongs to you, do not let yourself believe in the appearances, but declare divine order. You can trust God's perfect law of good. Divine order is being established now in your mind, body, and affairs through the power of the indwelling Christ. As you believe this truth, you will be free from doubt, fear, or anxiety and you will witness the wonderful ways in which God works to bless you and to bring forth good in you and in your life.

Problems in human relationships can arise because of lack of understanding between you and someone else. These problems can be helped and healed by declaring divine order, by believing in divine order. Where you may have been trying to restore peace through outer means, through personal efforts alone, you now see that all you need do is to let God take over in you and in everyone concerned.

To know that divine order is established frees you from feelings of unhappiness over what others may do or say. You are able to release, to bless, to forgive everyone. When you hold to the idea of divine order, you find that there are far fewer hurt feelings, far fewer arguments, far less friction in your association with others, for the idea of divine order, working through you, dissolves resistance and creates unity and harmony.

Chapter 9

An Astonishing Affirmation

At the age of ninety-four, Charles Fillmore, co-founder of Unity School, sat down and wrote out an affirmation for himself. It was found later among his papers and it was an astonishing affirmation for a man of any age: *I fairly sizzle with zeal and enthusiasm and spring forth with a mighty faith to do the things that ought to be done by me.*

Charles Fillmore always used lively words, words that created a feeling of action and power. At one time, when the mail in Silent Unity was particularly heavy and it did not seem that there were enough workers to handle it, he was asked to pray with Silent Unity. This is the affirmation he gave the workers: *I work with the speed and spring of Spirit!* Needless to say, the mail was handled promptly.

Affirmations are only words unless we give them life through our interest, feeling, and faith. Sometimes the very choice of words rekindles a new spirit in us, brings us to life, and we are able to speak our words with power and authority. We see instant results.

As you make your affirmations of Truth, never let your affirmations become routine. Never let the words become just memorized forms. Bring the words to life, put action into them. The Psalmist speaks of singing for joy before the Lord. We can, in a sense, sing for joy with the kind of prayers we make, with the words we use to enliven our minds, to stir up the spiritual powers that are in us.

Emerson said, "Nothing great was ever achieved without enthusiasm." All of us realize this, but too often we think of someone else as being naturally enthusiastic, as abounding in drive and energy. We accept ourselves as followers rather than initiators of action. We never feel that we are on fire with an idea, but we admire and marvel at the one who is.

Like Charles Fillmore, we can do something about our lack of enthusiasm. We can begin affirming just the opposite. We may feel that it is rather extreme to say that we "fairly sizzle with zeal and enthusiasm," but if we need a complete about-face, why not try using a word that has a shock value to it!

Paul tells us to "rekindle the gift of God that is within you" (2 Tim. 1:6). Each of us has the gift of God within. However, we are not always aware of the power that lies within us; we let its creative energy lie dormant and unused. Because we are capable of greater expressions of Truth than we are accomplishing, we feel vaguely restless and dissatisfied; we feel that there should be more to life. There should be, and there is! And our affirmations of Truth are the way to prove it. We are to rekindle the gift of God that is within us by affirming the Truth about ourselves. We are to call the sleeping self to life; we are to wake up the cells of the body, the brain; we are to come to life in Christ.

Take a few moments right now to look at yourself and your life. Ask yourself if you are accomplishing all that you are capable of accomplishing. Ask yourself if you are doing the things that need to be done by you. If you have thought that others are more capable or ready to do the things that need to be done, change your thought. Say to yourself, "I rekindle the gift of God that is within me." If you have felt that life is lacking in interest or enthusiasm, inject new life and spirit into your prayers and affirmations. Do not beg the Lord to change your life. Rather, make your strong, bold affirmation of spiritual power and ability, of zeal and enthusiasm, of springing, bounding joy.

Chapter 10

How Important Is It?

The trivial thing that upset you, the carelessly spoken word that hurt you—how important are they? They are as important as the attention you give them; they are as important as the unhappiness or distress they cause you.

Sometimes when our lives seem out of order, when it appears that we have one problem after another to meet, we wonder why we have to suffer or why things go wrong when we try so hard. We could well find a clue to our need by looking at ourselves objectively and discovering what we have allowed to assume importance in our thoughts and in our lives.

Healing may be delayed because we keep ourselves stirred up and irritated by the way others do or do not do what we expect of them. We may find ourselves cross, upset, and feeling sorry for ourselves because we think we are neglected, unappreciated, or misunderstood.

The things that annoy and upset us are important because they reveal a need in us to let go of the superficial and find the reality of Truth that underlies appearances.

If you have a problem that seems to be a constant source of worry and concern, try looking at it as objectively as possible. Try viewing it as a stranger would. Then ask yourself, "How important is it?" Is it more important than peace of mind? Is it more important than faith? Is it more important than God?

And what is faith? "Faith gives substance to our hopes and convinces us of realities we do not see" (Heb. 11:1 REB).

We would not be distressed or concerned by things around us, by other persons, by what seems to be failure and shortcoming if we did not instinctively believe that everyone and everything in God's world should be good and wonderful and perfect. We hope for perfection that we seldom seem to find. But mere hopefulness is shallow; it is disappointed; it is cast down because it looks at the appearance, the shadow, and sees it as the reality.

Faith is the spiritual side of hope. When we have faith, we do not just hope for the best, but we look at the things that appear, at the persons or the problems, at life, at ourselves, and we have eyes to see past appearances to the substance, the underlying good of God. We say to the appearance: "You are nothing. You are changing. You are passing. God endures. God, the goodness of God, is the one and only reality, and this is what I see, this is what I have faith in."

If we need healing, what is important? The temperature, the pulse rate, or the healing? Where we focus our thought and attention makes a difference in healing. Those who treat the sick say that some-times their patients get so enmeshed in symptoms, pains, and how they feel that they literally withdraw into a circumscribed world where the body and its demands receive their undivided attention. We need to give our thought and attention to the body in order to keep it well and strong, but the kind of thought and attention we give it makes a great differ-ence.

How differently we feel when we think of our bod-ies as temples of the living God, as the actual dwelling places of the Holy Spirit! How differently we feel when we realize that the life of God is strong in us, that there is only one life—God-life, and that this life flows through us as a mighty, healing, purify-ing, cleansing stream. Such thoughts are so inspiring and life-giving that we do not even want to talk about anything but life. We no longer attach importance to every little twinge or ache or pain. We declare life, we hold to life, we express life; and in doing so we are healed!

Some have clung to some hurt of the past or har-bored resentment and unforgiveness for years. How important is it? It is not important at all in God's sight! Anyone can learn to look at things from a spiritual viewpoint, can determine to lift her thoughts so that she sees as God sees. We live in the past as long as we carry it along with us, but we are not bound to it. We can let go and find freedom and newness when we stop dreaming about the past or regretting it, when we stop hoping for things to be as they once were, when we stand on faith and see the reality and goodness of God working through us and blessing us now.

Let us learn to ask ourselves when we are upset by anyone or anything, "How important is it?" How important is it in comparison to the Truth; how important is it when we remember that God is in and through all, that God's good is at work?

Everything in our lives can take on meaning and true importance as we have faith, the faith that "gives substance to our hopes and convinces us of realities we do not see."

Chapter 11

Meet It With Faith

Has something occurred to cause you grief or unhappiness? Meet it with faith, the faith that God is with you, the faith that God is present in every person and in every situation, the faith that God can be trusted to bless, to renew, to heal, and to make all things right.

Meet it with faith! This is the way to overcome unhappiness. As you look past what seems to be and hold to the Truth that nothing can separate you from God's love, nothing can cast you down, nothing is greater than God's power in you, cares slip away, and the joy of Spirit rises up in you.

The often surprising result of holding to faith is the great welling up of faith that you feel within you. When you take your stand and declare, *I have faith in God as the one Presence and the one Power, the one life, the one healer,* there is an answering response within you. It is as though God says within you: "I am here. I am your life. I am your being. I am your all." You feel a new faith, stronger and more certain than any you have known before. And with this faith comes healing. "Your faith has made you well" (Mt. 9:22).

Do you ever find yourself wondering how you are going to meet your bills or where the money is coming from? Meet such thoughts with faith. Stand up to your doubts and fears. Vanquish them with the bright light of faith. Who is your source? Who is the supplier of every needed good? God. And where is God? Right within you, the Fountainhead of your good, the Source of all your supply. Have faith in the substance of God to provide for your every need, abundantly, perfectly.

The faith you have in the invisible but all-providing Spirit will bring forth results in outer ways that will sometimes be astonishing. You can prove God as your source and your supply as you meet every appearance of lack, every thought of lack with faith—faith that is strong and unwavering, faith that calls forth God, calls forth the power of good, and sets God's wonderful Spirit to work in and through you.

How do you meet disappointment? If you have met it with tears or angry protests, you know how unrewarding this way has been; you know how it only adds frustration to frustration. To meet disappointment with faith is to lift up your thoughts to God and to rise to the place in consciousness where you can say: *There is no disappointment. There is only God, only good. I see God in myself; I see God's good in everyone and everything. I know that all things are working together for good.*

How can there be unhappiness or disappointment when we know that there is underlying good at work? Any one of us can look back and recall how

43

something that seemed a great disappointment at the time turned out to be a blessing in disguise. We can see now that only our lack of understanding and spiritual vision at the time kept us from beholding God's good plan at work for us.

Even when it seems that we are misunderstood, unfairly treated, or unjustly condemned, let us not believe in the appearances. "Do not be overcome by evil, but overcome evil with good" (Rom. 12:21). Do you remember what Joseph said to his brothers? "Even though you intended to do harm to me, God intended it for good" (Gen. 50:20). In every circumstance and situation have faith that God means it for good. Have faith in God's power, love, and justice. Do not believe that you or anyone else can be separated from God's loving care or that God's law of justice can be overthrown.

Negation has no power. It can have no power over you and no place in your heart or thoughts or life as you meet all things with faith, faith in God, faith in God's power, faith in the sure outworking of divine good.

"Now faith is the assurance of things hoped for, the conviction of things not seen.... By faith we understand that the worlds were prepared by the word of God, so that what is seen was made from things that are not visible" (Heb. 11:1, 3).

Whatever the appearance, meet it with faith!

Part III

Healing

Chapter 12

You Have Healing Power

Most of us do not think of ourselves as having spiritual power or as being able to heal or help ourselves or anyone else. When a need arises, we turn to someone whom we think of as spiritual, as a man or woman of God, as a minister.

But if there is no one to turn to and we find ourselves forced to meet some situation alone, are we helpless, are we without power?

Think of how the disciples of Jesus felt when He was no longer with them. He had told them that they could do the things He did and even greater; He had told them that He would be with them always; He had instructed them to ask in His name, that the Father might be glorified. But without the actual presence of Jesus, the disciples must have felt small and inadequate; indeed, they must have wondered how they could carry on the great work, how they could fulfill the vision that Jesus Christ had given them. They did not realize the power that was with them, within them, until they used it, invoked it, called it forth.

"One day Peter and John were going up to the temple at the hour of prayer, at three o'clock in the afternoon. And a man lame from birth was being carried in. People would lay him daily at the gate of the temple called the Beautiful Gate so that he could ask for alms from those entering the temple. When he saw Peter and John about to go into the temple, he asked them for alms. Peter looked intently at him, as did John, and said, 'Look at us.' And he fixed his attention on them, expecting to receive something from them. But Peter said, 'I have no silver or gold, but what I have I give you; in the name of Jesus Christ of Nazareth, stand up and walk.' And he took him by the right hand and raised him up; and immediately his feet and ankles were made strong. Jumping up, he stood and began to walk, and he entered the temple with them, walking and leaping and praising God" (Acts 3:1-8).

Peter and John spoke the word of faith and healing in the name and through the power of Jesus Christ of Nazareth. They knew that the power to heal was not in their human efforts but in God. They knew also that this power could be called forth through faith, and that they were the men of faith needed at that particular moment.

When we pray in the name and through the power of Jesus Christ, is it the mere pronouncement of the name that heals, that transforms, that blesses? No, it is what we experience when we pray in the name of Jesus Christ. Jesus said, "Where two or three are gathered in my name, I am there among them" (Mt. 18:20). When even one person prays in the name of Jesus Christ, he invokes the living presence of the loving Christ. We are not alone when we pray in the name of Jesus Christ; He is with us, His presence and power are with us, and the power that is of God flows through us. It is said that certain disciples were so conscious of the Christ with them that even the shadows they cast had healing power. They did not claim the power as theirs; they did not claim personal glory; for they knew, as Jesus knew and taught, that God is the power.

If you have longed for more light, for more spiritual power, for a truer realization of God's presence, invoke the power that is in you by calling it forth in the name and through the power of Jesus Christ. Do not think that you have to wait until you have more faith in order to help another or to heal another. The power is not personal power; the power that lies in you is God-power, and this power is released through faith.

Every time you pray, every time you look past the appearances and see God at work, you are using your faith; and God acts through your faith. God needs you to say: "This can be healed. All things are possible. There is nothing incurable."

God's work is done by the faithful and the fearless. You are one of these, for you are a child of God. God has put His Spirit in you, God has poured out His power upon you.

Chapter 13

God Is Your Life

There is within you a strong, compelling will to live. With every breath you affirm life, and with every heartbeat you take your stand for life. Nothing can defeat the life in you, for it is of God. It is without beginning or end; it is the eternal life in which you live, move, and have your being.

The appearance of disease or disorder in the body cannot impair the life of God in you. Rather, it is the knowledge of God's life as part of the fiber of your being that rises up to challenge the appearance of disease, that marshals the forces of your being, that says *no* to negation, fear, or belief in imperfection.

If ever you feel that you are weak in your hold on life, that you are not strong enough in faith to proclaim healing, or that some condition is too serious or of too long-standing to respond to prayer, then you need to remind yourself that it is God in you who is strong. It is God in you who does the healing work. It is God in you who supplies you with life—renewing, revitalizing life.

Affirm to yourself: *I am strong in the Lord.* Think about what this means. You are strong in the Lord, so your strength is of God. It is not a strength that depends on externals or a strength that you sometimes have, but a strength that you always have. You are strong in the Lord. You are a part of the life of God, for your body is spiritual in nature. It is created of the very substance of God. "Do you not know that you are God's temple and that God's Spirit dwells in you?" (1 Cor. 3:16) You are strong in the Lord, and the Lord is strong in you. Knowing this, you are sustained at all times by an inner strength. You are upheld by an inner power, and you are revitalized and made alive.

God is mighty in you to vitalize, renew, and heal you. What you cannot do through your own efforts or through an act of will, God does easily and effortlessly in and through you. If you have been trying to will your way to health and wholeness, let go and let God work through you. Let go and lean on the Presence, mighty in the midst of you. Know that you do not have to strain after health, for God is with you as health. You do not of yourself re-create, renew, or revitalize your body. God is the life; God is the renewer; God is the revitalizer. You are the perfect and willing channel through which God works. You are the open mind; you are the receptive heart; you are the calm, relaxed instrument through which the life of God is steadily poured forth and through which the perfection of God is constantly maintained.

"I praise you, for I am fearfully and
wonderfully made.
Wonderful are your works;
that I know very well."
—Psalm 139:14

51

You are "fearfully and wonderfully made." Wonderful are the works of God in you. The power of God in you is greater than your mind can imagine; the strength of God in you is greater than any demand you have yet made on it, either in mind or body. You are strong in the Lord.

Chapter 14

True Healing Does Not Depend on Time

In a very real sense we are renewed continually—mentally, physically, and spiritually. Sometimes, just to realize this truth is all that we need in order to be healed and set free.

We may understand that we can think new thoughts and attain new spiritual insights, but we may not be able to accept the idea of newness for our bodies. We think of it as being subject to physical laws. If we have some condition that is termed chronic, we often fail to think in terms of newness and healing of the condition. We more often pray to be able to live with it.

When Jesus healed, He did not differentiate between the kinds of illnesses He healed. He healed the mind; He healed the body; He healed those who had suddenly become sick; He healed those who had been ill for years, those who had been blind from birth, crippled for years; He healed the woman with the illness of long standing, who had the faith merely to touch the hem of His garment.

True healing is not determined by time as we know it. True healing does not depend on the nature of the disease or its duration. True healing is not limited by the pattern that has always seemed to run true with a particular condition. True healing is of God, from God, and is the return, in a flash, in an instant—in the eternity that is God's time—to the perfection in which we were created.

When God breathed Spirit into the nostrils of the first human being, a living soul was born. God looked on this creation and saw it as good. God still looks on us and sees us as good. God does not see the illness, the hurts, the imperfections; God's love sees only the perfect child of God. The creative Spirit that breathed us into life in the first place is continually pouring life through us, is continually renewing us, and is continually healing us, if we are only aware of it.

We do have faith in life, whether we know it or not. The fact that we are alive, that we live and draw breath, is faith in action. With every breath we draw, with every beat of our heart, we are proclaiming life and affirming life. We are saying, "God lives in me, I live in God."

What we need to let go of entirely are our old ways of thinking that are limited, that are fearful, that are anxious, that are filled with belief in the power of disease, that give power to the condition rather than God. We need to get rid of our old ways of talking about ourselves and others.

Sometimes we find that a person is still talking about how he felt, how he suffered, how he was at the mercy of some disease years and years ago. We like to dramatize ourselves and our experiences. We like to command the attention and the sympathy of others, and sometimes we attempt to do this by reminding ourselves and others continually of the things that happened to us in the past.

We are creatures of habit, and we do not always realize the kind of thought habits or speech habits we have formed. We need to watch our thinking and speaking and guard against any stress on the old, the negative, the morbid, the sad. We are living children of the living God, and we can rise up in newness of life and light; we can enter into a new and vital way of life. This new and vital way of life is what we really want, for it is our nature. It is our destiny as children of God to be free, to be marvelously and wonderfully alive, and to be aware of the light, power, and love of God filling us and moving through us.

Chapter 15

Do You Want to Be Healed?

There is a great desire on the part of all people to be well, happy, and strong. This desire is present in every one of us, because we were created for life; our right and natural state is health and well-being.

People will try almost anything that promises to give them more life and vitality, because they have an instinctive belief in health.

While all of us desire life and health, sometimes this desire is clouded over or even superseded by our desire for love and understanding, by our need to feel cared for, by our desire for attention. If we have been surrounded by much love and attention because of illness or if we have become dependent on others, our desire for healing and a return to normal, responsible living may be weakened. Without our being consciously aware of it, we may have actually accepted sickness as a way of life. But in our inmost selves we are in conflict, for the desire to live and the desire to stand strong and free is greater than the desire for ease and comfort and sympathy.

The will to live is in us all, and we are not happy or

at peace within ourselves when we are not express-ing this will of God in us. Though everyone else praises us for endurance and patience under suffer-ing, we want more than patience and endurance; we want life, the life abundant that Jesus promised.

We have in us not only the desire to be well and the will to live, but also the strength to resist the temptation to settle for sympathy when what we really want is strength. The strength to resist the inclination to give way to self-pity, the strength to give way to God so that God's healing work can be done in us and through us.

Faith on our part transforms innate desire, innate will into an active force, a vitalizing, healing power. We no longer just feel in a vague way that we should be well and strong; we put ourselves actively into this belief. We declare our faith, live our faith, use our faith, stand by our faith. We take our stand for heal-ing, and we know where we stand.

We know without doubt or wavering that we choose to live. We do not wonder any longer if it is God's will for us to be healed. We do not try to make sickness into a virtue. We remember the words of Jehovah, spoken through Ezekiel, "For I have no pleasure in the death of anyone .... Turn, then, and live" (Ezek. 18:32).

We know that the desire in us for life and health is there, because we are meant for life. We turn away from belief in sickness or disease and from the belief that we cannot be healed, and we make our every thought, word, and prayer an affirmation of life. This is faith in action—to believe in God, to believe in life, to believe in healing, and to keep on believing.

"If the Spirit of him who raised Jesus from the dead dwells in you, he who raised Christ from the dead will give life to your mortal bodies also through his Spirit that dwells in you" (Rom. 8:11).

The Spirit that gives life to our mortal bodies is in us. It is the life of God, the animating force of our being. This is what we need to realize above all else in our search for health: that health comes from Spirit. The life that flows through us from Spirit is life without beginning or end, life that is free and pure and perfect, life that cannot be weakened by disease. It is powerful, perfect, ceaseless, changeless—and it is within us. We have every reason to believe that we can be healed; we have every reason to have faith; and we have every reason to refuse to believe that any condition is beyond help or healing.

Do you want to be healed? Your desire for health and strength and newness of life comes from God. The will to be well comes from God, and the Spirit that performs the healing miracles is not far from you. It is within you, it is God's own life-giving Spirit, mighty in the midst of you.

You are created of the very substance of God, and the pattern of life is hidden in every cell. The call to life is heard and felt by every part of you. You can be healed, for you are right now filled with God's Spirit. You are right now partaking of God's life.

Chapter 16

A Healing Treatment

All healing is spiritual; all healing comes from God. Jesus emphasized again and again that our part in healing is faith, belief, and receptivity.

We increase our faith, belief, and receptivity through the practice of prayer. Prayer brings us into the presence of God. Prayer opens our entire beings to the inflow of divine love, to the inrush of healing life, and to the power of the Holy Spirit.

There are many ways of prayer. Not method but willingness of heart and spirit is what is important in prayer. There are no set formulas for effective prayer or no rules that must be followed in order to achieve results, for prayer is not a form but a force. It is the need in us to find and know the healing, the answer, the reason for our being—to know ourselves in God, to know God in us.

The following healing treatment is presented for those who are seeking help in increasing their faith, belief, and receptivity—those who are seeking to lay hold on the spiritual life-force that flows freely and ceaselessly from God.

A Healing Treatment

1. Relaxation: The first thing to do is to *relax.* Before beginning this treatment, choose a comfortable place where you can be alone and free from interruption. Choose a comfortable chair. Sit quietly with your eyes closed and relax. Unclench your fists, let go of tension, relax. Sit quietly for a few minutes, then say to yourself, "Be still, and know that I am God!" (Ps. 46:10) God is with you right now. Right now you are in the Presence; right now God's love enfolds you; right now God's peace surrounds you. Be still! Say to yourself, "Relax and let go. Underneath are the everlasting arms." Your mind, body, and emotions will feel the soothing effect of relaxation. This is the first step toward receptivity.

2. Denial: The next necessary step to realizing healing is the *denial* of belief in illness, disease, negation of any kind. The best kind of denial is a sweeping one, the denial that says to negation, "You are nothing. You have no power." It says in the face of disease, "There is no disease" and proclaims, "There is no pain." Denial is a washing away of your belief in appearances, pain, and disease. It is the housecleaning that makes ready for newness and healing. True denial is not negative but positive. It is a positive declaration of your faith in life, in God, in perfection. Denial is a way of saying to your doubts, your fears, your belief that disease has power, "I do not believe it!"

3. Affirmation: To use denial to sweep your mental

house clean of belief in negation is necessary, but it should always be followed by strong, bold *affirmations* of Truth. Denial prepares the way. Affirmation carries you forward to a new awareness of life, of power, of a new awareness of the presence of God in whom you live and move and have your being. After denying the reality of disease, affirm the reality of God. You can make your affirmation along lines such as this: *There is only the life of God flowing freely through me from the top of my head to the soles of my feet, cleansing, purifying, healing, vitalizing, renewing, and restoring me.*

This life stream, this life-force, is mighty in the midst of you. Everything in you works toward life and wholeness when your mind is free from fear and when you are an unobstructed channel through which Spirit can pour. When you affirm God's power, you identify yourself with it; when you affirm God's life, you identify yourself with it. When you identify yourself with God, you enter into the healing Christ life; you become one with the very life and substance of God. The Word becomes flesh and dwells within you, life of your life, breath of your breath.

4. Realization: Relaxation, denial, affirmation—these are followed by the fourth step, which is *realization*. Realization goes beyond thought, beyond words; it is the incorporation into your being of God, the incorporation into your body of the living substance of Spirit; it is the bread and wine made flesh and blood; it is the inner knowing that comes to you, the glory that shines through you. With realization comes a radiance, an inward glow. You do not wonder if God has heard your prayer. You *know*! You stand in the light of God's presence. Your eyes are opened to the Truth, and new life surges through you. New faith carries you forward.

5. Thankfulness: The great amen to every prayer is a welling up of *thankfulness* in your heart. You are not thanking God for favors requested or favors granted, but you are thanking God over and over for what God is and for what you are. Thankfulness is more than saying, "Thank You, God." It is the giving over of your whole self, your whole life to God. It is the joyous abandonment of self-will, the relinquishing of the little self, the petty life and ways, to the larger will and the happier ways of Spirit. Your thankful heart praises God with every thought, word, and act. Like the Psalmist you say, "Bless the Lord, O my soul, and all that is within me, bless his holy name" (Ps. 103:1).

Part IV

You Are an Influence for Good

Chapter 17

Can You Get Along With Yourself?

Emmet Fox once said that if a person could not get along with other people, he should make a sign and hang it inside his closet, where he would see it every day. This sign was to read, "Like attracts like."

It usually seems as though it is the other person who should change or that it is the other person about whom something should be done. But like attracts like. So if we cannot get along with others, we may need to do some changing ourselves.

Those who cannot get along with others usually cannot get along with themselves either. They are unhappy with the way they think and feel. They criticize and condemn themselves more severely than they do anyone else.

To learn to get along better with oneself may not seem to be the key to getting along with others, but it is. It may not be possible for us to change someone else, but the one person we can work with, the one person we can change, is ourself. Since it is always more feasible to work with the possible rather than the impossible, this is where we need to begin, not with the other person but with ourselves.

Have you ever thought about what kind of attitudes and reactions you have? Are they loving, are they kind, are they tolerant, are they encouraging? How do you feel inside most of the time? Are you resentful, unforgiving, or jealous? You need not answer these questions to anyone but yourself. You are the only one who knows the inner you. But sometimes, even you do not really know yourself, and you are not aware perhaps of how the tenor of your thoughts and feelings may have become negative or depressed.

If you try to change your attitudes and feelings by determination or willpower, you will probably not get very far. The secret of transformation, the secret of change, is to begin with prayer. The changes you want to bring about are not of the outer but of the inner, and it is the power of God that quickens the inner being.

God's Spirit is in you. You are created in God's image and likeness, and prayer brings you back to the remembrance of this. The best, the only way to change you, is to find out who you are, what you are, what you are meant to express, what you are meant to be.

When we want to change the way we think, feel, and react, prayer is the beginning and the prayer to begin with is a prayer for light. When we pray for light, we do not have to beg God for it any more than we have to beg the sun to shine. The light of Spirit is already shining within us. What then does our prayer do? Our prayer opens our eyes, our hearts, our minds, our spirits to the light. The darkness that has hung over us is lifted. We see ourselves in the light of Truth.

To know and understand ourselves, we need to know that we are essentially spiritual beings. Because we are, we are never satisfied with ourselves when we do not express the inner Godlike qualities that we intuitively know we possess. How can we change our feelings and our thoughts into those that make us feel right inside, happy and satisfied with ourselves? We can center ourselves in the loving Christ presence; "take every thought captive to obey Christ" (2 Cor. 10:5). When our thoughts are Christ-directed and Christ-inspired, they are love-directed, and they are love-inspired. To follow Christ in thought and feeling, in action and reaction, in word and deed, is to follow the way of love, light, peace, growth, and joy.

Chapter 18

You Are an Influence for Good

Most of us would be astonished if we were shown how great an influence we exert on the lives of others. But if we consider our own selves, we know this is true. Do you find yourself recalling something that someone said to you, perhaps years ago, that influenced you in some direction, possibly to the extent of changing your life? This other person may or may not remember the incident at all and would most likely find it difficult to remember the exact words spoken to you—words that you have never forgotten, words that have been engraved on your heart and mind.

All of us are influenced not only by the words of others but by being around those who bring out qualities in us that we did not know we possessed. We love those who somehow make us feel worthy and in whose presence we feel alive and encouraged.

As parents, teachers, employers, or friends, we may sometimes wish that we could influence another. We see a child going in a direction that would seem to lead to unhappiness or frustration. We try talking without getting the response we hope for; in fact, our talking may only tend to alienate this child further from us. How can we be an influence for good? The greatest influence we have on anyone—child, student, or friend—is the influence of our own lives as we live them and the influence we exert in being ourselves.

When we pray for another, we place her in God's care. We see her as God's child; we behold the perfect Self of her, the God Self. We affirm her perfection in God; we give thanks that God is within her, that God is her life, her strength, her light, her power, her all in all.

If we attempt through prayer to influence another person to our way of thinking or believing, we are usually disappointed. But when we pray for another in faith and love, we keep our faith centered in the power of God, the Good, and know that God is present in all concerns. This prayer cannot help but bless the one for whom we pray. There is a spark of divinity in everyone, and prayer reaches through to the inner being, and quickens her awareness of Spirit within.

When you think about the people who have influenced you most and have had an impact for good on your life, is it not true that they are the ones who gave you the most freedom to learn and grow in your own way? They were the ones who believed in you and helped you to believe in yourself.

A good teacher does not try to cram knowledge into the brain of a student. Rather, he encourages the student to listen and learn; he inspires her to think for herself, to discover and call forth the innate powers and abilities that are already within her.

Jesus said, "Let your light shine before others, so that they may see your good works and give glory to your Father in heaven" (Mt. 5:16). Each one of us is the light of the world. We may wonder how this can be; we may not feel like a bearer of light, but we are. We let our lights shine by letting God's light shine in us and through us. God is light. God is the light of our minds, the light of our spirits, the light of our world. As we live in the conscious awareness of God's presence, as we walk in God's light, we do not need to concern ourselves with letting our light shine before humanity. Centered in God, we become radiating centers of divine light and life, mighty to attract our good and to radiate good to others.

The Bible is filled with marvelous references to light, beginning with the creation in Genesis when God said, " 'Let there be light'; and there was light." And what shining words the following ones are for all of us; "Arise, shine; for your light has come, and the glory of the Lord has risen upon you" (Is. 60:1). "For once you were darkness, but now in the Lord you are light. Live as children of light—for the fruit of the light is found in all that is good and right and true" (Eph. 5:8-9).

It has been said that there is not enough darkness in the whole world to put out the light of one small candle. You may think of yourself and your life as insignificant or unimportant, but you are a light in the world. You are needed; you are an influence for good.

Through your faith and prayers you are blessed and you radiate a blessing to others.

Chapter 19

Overcome Evil With Good

No one is happy or at peace who lives under a cloud of criticism or condemnation. If we have to live with or work with someone who continually criticizes or belittles us or who finds fault with what we do and the way we do it, what is the answer? How shall we find freedom from this particular situation?

In Romans we read, "Do not repay anyone evil for evil, but take thought for what is noble in the sight of all. If it is possible, so far as it depends on you, live peaceably with all. Beloved, never avenge yourselves, but leave room for ... God; for ... 'I will repay, says the Lord.... If your enemies are hungry, feed them; if they are thirsty, give them something to drink....' Do not be overcome by evil, but overcome evil with good" (Rom. 12:17-21).

If we meet criticism with criticism, we are rendering evil for evil. To meet criticism and condemnation in a spirit of love is to overcome evil with good. When we meet criticism and condemnation in a spirit of love, we do more than insure our own peace of mind; we reach out to bless even our so-called enemy, we "leave room for ... God," that is, we bring God into the situation.

One of the most helpful affirmations of Truth that we can take for ourselves is: *There is no criticism or condemnation in me, for me, or against me. I am under the law of divine love, and all is well with me and my world.*

The person we always have to work with is ourself. "If it is possible, so far as it depends on you, live peaceably with all." So if we are working to free ourselves from a critical, unhappy atmosphere, let us begin with ourself, our own thoughts, our own feelings, and our own reactions. *There is no criticism or condemnation in me.* We can open our minds to divine love and forgiveness and let the forgiving, healing power of God's love bless our thoughts and set us free from every trace of animosity or resentment. We forgive and free all persons in our thoughts of them. *There is no criticism or condemnation in me.*

Even if there are persons around us who seem to find fault or who blame or condemn us unjustly, then, because our hearts are filled with forgiving love, we can affirm: *There is no criticism or condemnation in me, for me, or against me. I am under the law of divine love, and all is well with me and my world.*

When we take this idea—namely, that we are under the law of divine love—and live with it, abide in it, make it our continual realization, we find that where before we seemed to live under a cloud of criticism, now this cloud is lifted, and we are in the light. We live in a spiritual atmosphere, an atmosphere of freedom, an atmosphere of peace, an atmosphere of well-being.

To know that we live under the law of divine love

and that all is well with us and our world lifts any feelings of guilt or anxiety from our minds and hearts. If we have allowed ourselves to feel inadequate or inferior or if we have listened to negative criticism instead of listening to the Spirit of God in the midst of us, we need to be still, to pray for light, and to let God's Spirit in us fill us anew with faith and power, with Truth and light.

Negative situations always call for positive actions. Let us remember this in any time of difficulty or inharmony. The most positive action we can take is the action of prayer, the prayer that affirms the presence of God and the underlying goodness of God, the prayer that beholds the Spirit of God at work in all people and all situations.

We may be amazed at the way people and situations seem to change when we pray about them and for them, but we should not be amazed, for always the good is there, and always the power of good is greater than negation.

Whenever you are tempted to be depressed or unhappy because of what someone has said or done, use this affirmation: *There is no criticism or condemnation in me, for me, or against me. I am under the law of divine love, and all is well with me and my world.* You will find how great is the strength and power and help in this prayer.

Chapter 20

Not What You Say, but How You Say It

"I didn't mind so much what she said, it was the way she said it!"

You have heard this kind of remark time and again—probably you have made it yourself upon occasion.

What we say is important, but even more important is how we say it.

Two persons can make almost identical remarks: one person's remarks will be accepted in good spirit, while the other person's remarks will rankle the hearer, perhaps offend or cause hurt feelings.

What is the difference between the what and the how in this matter of expressing ourselves? The difference lies in inner motivation, the feeling we project through our words. How we feel makes a difference in how our words sound to others and how they react to them. If we are critical or envious of another person, our seemingly innocent remark may be disturbing and upsetting, for what we say is overshadowed by what we feel. The discordant note sounds, even though we seem to be playing the right music.

How many times a person will say of someone, "I know she's right, but it's the way she says it that upsets me." The nagging wife may be ever so right in her suggestions to her long-suffering husband, but usually he hears in her voice only complaint and criticism rather than the soundness or rightness of her ideas. The parent who continually harps on a child's failures or shortcomings may think he is only trying to be helpful. However, the child usually does not hear the positive or good ideas; the child hears only the complaints, the voice of parental disappointment.

Our words are important. What we say is important, but even more important is the way we think, the way we feel, and the way we react to people and to life in general.

If you are not happy in your relationships with other people or if you find yourself becoming upset or upsetting others when you try to get your ideas across, perhaps your need is to get back to God, to re-establish your relationship with God, and to find yourself in God.

When your faith is firmly fixed in God and in God's good, you approach life from a new standpoint; you see the situations and the persons in your life through new eyes. When you try to change conditions or people through your personal efforts or will, it is usually a disappointing, frustrating business. But waiting patiently on God and opening your mind and heart and entire being to Spirit's inspiration is a lifting, renewing experience. The more you let your mind be filled with positive true ideas, the more you dwell on the goodness of God, the more solid is your foundation of faith and trust. Your feet are set upon a rock and all your comings and goings are established.

Right here is where you learn the difference between what you say and how you say it. For when your thoughts are centered in God, when you see the Spirit of God at work in you, in your life, and in the people around you, then you have a new song, a song of praise unto your God.

A song of praise unto God in your heart charges the words that you speak with new meaning. When your heart and mind are filled with praise to God, then the words you speak are life-giving, peace-producing, and the words you speak inspire and encourage, instruct and bless.

The Truth of God is within you, and as you base your thinking on Truth you will find that your words are words of Truth. Sometimes people seek everywhere for Truth except where it is to be found, in the inner realms of being, the secret place of the Most High within them. If ever you wonder how you are to know the Word of God, how you are to find the Truth, remember that "the word is very near to you; it is in your mouth and in your heart for you to observe" (Deut. 30:14).

Chapter 21

Give, Give, and Give Again

We look at other people and think that they are free from the doubts and fears that assail us; we cannot imagine that they feel as unsure of themselves, as lacking in confidence, as we do.

The more we know and understand people, the more we see that the need to feel accepted, approved of, or loved is universal.

Young people are so dominated by the desire to be accepted and popular, that they often make themselves and others unhappy by trying to be something they are not; they imitate and copy those who seem to have what they want. They do not appreciate their own worth; they underrate themselves. They do not realize that the way to approval and acceptance is not found through some application of personality, but through bringing forth and using the qualities that are in them, the qualities that make them unique and necessary and, when used, assure them of their own unchallenged place in the world.

Jesus said, "Give, and it will be given to you" (Lk. 6:38). This applies to giving in all its phases and forms. We cannot give without receiving. This does not mean an exact return from the one to whom we have given. It means that when we give we fulfill the law, and the return comes, sometimes in ways that we expect, oftentimes in unexpected and wonderful ways that we could not have imagined or anticipated.

If for some reason we feel rejected, unwanted, or unloved, the sure way out of this unhappy state is to give. We may ask, "What can I give? What have I to give?"

To answer these questions, we should ask ourselves, "What is it that I want? What would make me happy?" If we want love and approval, "give, and it will be given to you." We can give love and approval to someone, to some degree. We can speak words of praise and appreciation that we may have withheld before.

If we want love and friendship, we can remember the instruction: "Give, and it will be given to you." We may say, "But this *is* my problem. I find it difficult to be friendly. I find it hard to be loving toward others." This is the beginning point, then. We can make what may seem small efforts at first to express friendly feelings toward others.

We need to begin with the way we think and feel about others. If we have felt critical or envious of others, our giving can be the giving of our blessing to them in our own minds. If we have felt timid and unsure of ourselves in the presence of others, our giving can be the giving up of fear. In outer ways, we can give of ourselves through our willingness to help others, a willingness to listen to others that springs from a willingness to let go of our own self-centeredness long enough to really see other people as being like us, as having needs and desires that are similar to ours, as longing to know us better, even as we long to feel closer and freer in our relations with them.

Jesus also said, "Those who lose their life for my sake will find it" (Mt. 10:39). To lose our lives in Christ is to let go of concentration on self, on what we want or desire, and to rise into a higher place in thought where we see ourselves as spiritual, as having Christ in us, where we see that to begin with Christ is to find life. We see that we have been trying to put on something from the outside; we have been trying to do or be something that seemed to us good and desirable, but the true Self in us is discovered as we let the Christ nature take over in us. To lose our lives is to let go of striving and straining. It is to let go of the little self so that the larger Self, the Christ, may emerge, may take over in us. This is to find ourselves, to find our lives. It is another way of fulfilling the law of giving and receiving.

Sometimes when we feel rejected and unloved it is not so much because other people reject us or do not love us, but because we reject ourselves; we do not love and appreciate ourselves. To accept ourselves, to love and appreciate ourselves is not egotism—those who seem the most egotistical actually are trying to prove their worth to themselves and everyone else.

To accept and appreciate ourselves we need to become aware of ourselves in our true nature. Who are we? What are we? Each of us is a child of God, created in God's image and likeness, beloved of God, important to God, needed by God.

When we have walked in loneliness and unhappiness, we may feel that we have wasted the years, that our lives do not count for much. "Give, and it will be given to you" means also to give up negative and depressing ideas like this. As we do, the way is opened for God's light to brighten every corner of our lives and to transform and bless us, to renew and restore us, to give us new insight so that we see that nothing is lost or wasted, that it is never too late to begin to give; it is never too late to receive our good.

When we feel the need to be accepted, approved of, or loved, it is the prompting of God's Spirit in us, saying: "Give, give, and give again. This is the way of love and light and joy. This is the way to newness of life."

Chapter 22

A Cheerful Heart Is a Good Medicine

If we find it difficult to have a cheerful heart, if we are nervous or depressed, if we feel that we are in emotional conflict, what can we do about it? No two persons are exactly alike; no one else's needs are exactly the same as ours; no one else reacts to life in just the same manner that we do; still, there are basic principles of thinking and acting, of attitude and reaction that apply to all of us and can be used with good results by any of us.

If we would have cheerful hearts, we cannot allow feelings of unforgiveness to remain. We may think that we are not harboring unforgiveness, but if we consciously or unconsciously blame anyone or anything for our unhappiness, we have a need to forgive. When we think about the love of God, we know that it is all embracing, all forgiving. And the love that is in us is from God.

Forgiveness is not difficult when we realize that it is through the love of God in us that we are able to forgive. It is through the love of God that we are able to release the hurts of the past, that we are able to drop from our consciousness the memories that have gnawed at our peace of mind, that have rankled our souls. It is through letting the love of God find expression through us that we are able to let go of suppressed anger, that our hurt feelings are released and healed. The pent-up emotions are set free, the anger is dissolved through the balm of healing love that we allow to flow freely.

Sometimes depressed and destructive feelings build up in us, because we are trying too hard, personally, to take control. The frustration felt is like that experienced when trying to drive a car with the brakes on. We can learn to relax, to let go of our tense hold on ourselves, on our lives, on other persons. The way we do this is to remind ourselves continually that God is with us, that it is through the Spirit in us that we are able to do all things. Paul said, "I can do all things through him who strengthens me" (Phil. 4:13). This is a good thing for us to remember.

We are not at the mercy of our moods; we can help being the way we are. We are not moody or quick-tempered because we inherited our dispositions from someone in the family. We are this way only because we have let ourselves build up this habit of action and reaction, but we have it in our power to change. Once we believe that we can be the way we want to be, once we take this stand, we have made definite progress. We have taken a real step toward controlling our moods, toward improving our dispositions.

Often we think that we could keep cheerful and

happy and have good dispositions if other people were different, if they were easier to get along with, if they would not do upsetting things, if they did not say hurtful or unkind things. But the truth we need to face is that the only change needed in order for us to be peaceful and happy is in our own thinking, in our own attitudes. The surprising thing is that once we have begun to work with ourselves, once we have begun to rely on the Spirit of God in us to inspire us, to direct us, to speak through us, to act through us, and to love through us, those around us seem different in our eyes. We can look at them with love and compassion.

We learn to have cheerful hearts when we learn where to place our dependence. As long as we are overly dependent on others, we find ourselves hurt and let down when they do not measure up to our expectations of them. When we place our dependence in God, we are starting on a sure and stable foundation. We should bless and love others for their part in our lives, for the ways in which they contribute to our happiness and well-being; but we should not put them in God's place, we should not look to them for our good, our guidance, our answers. As we go to God first in all things, we become stronger and more self-assured. We are able to maintain our thoughts and feelings on an even, happy keel.

A cheerful heart can be cultivated; it is not something that some people have that we cannot hope to have. We can learn to work with ourselves, with our thoughts, with our feelings, with our moods, with our problems. We can learn to have faith in God and in the good, and it is this faith that enables us to meet life with a strong and spontaneous, but quiet, flow of good spirits.

> "A cheerful heart is a good medicine,
> but a downcast spirit dries up the bones."
> —Proverbs 17:22

Chapter 23

Do You Pray for Others?

Do you realize that every time you think of others with love and faith you are blessing them, that every time you think of others as having the Spirit of God in them, you are praying for them?

This is the secret of effective prayers in behalf of others: to love and have faith in those for whom you pray, to see the Spirit of God in them.

Now, as you read these words, some person may come to mind who needs help in some way. As you think of this person, do you feel loving? If you do not, then this is your first need before you pray, to lift your heart and mind to God, to let the love of God fill you and express itself through you toward this one for whom you would pray. There is not any person in the whole world whom you cannot love, when you love as God loves, when you see all persons as children of God, as one with you in Spirit, indeed, as a very part of you.

Jesus said, "When you are offering your gift at the altar, if you remember that your brother or sister has something against you, leave your gift there before the altar and go; first be reconciled to your brother or sister, and then come and offer your gift" (Mt. 5:23-24). We may be praying for someone who is thousands of miles from us. How can we go and be reconciled with this person before continuing our prayers?

We go in thought; we change our thought about this person. We let go of any thought of dislike, disapproval, unforgiveness, jealousy, or bitterness. We let the love of God cleanse our hearts and then we are able to pour out love, then we are able to pray, for we have done away with the separation we have built up between ourselves and others, between ourselves and God.

Even when we are filled with love for the one for whom we would pray, sometimes this very love makes us too concerned, too emotional, too sympathetic to be positive in our thoughts and feelings. We want to be sensitive, understanding, and compassionate. But we also want to be strong and sure in our faith that the power of God dwells in the one for whom we pray. Our love needs to be linked with our faith.

Sometimes we find it easier to pray for ourselves than for others, because when we pray for ourselves, even though we may not see the way, we have a sure sense that God will open the way. What we need to remember as we pray for others is that they have the Spirit of God in them, they have an inner light, an innate faith; they have something in them that gives them faith and assurance.

We should never wish that we could step in and live another's life for him, solve his problems for him. He can do this for himself, and far better than we or anyone else can, for God is with him, and God can be trusted to be his light and guide.

Whenever you pray for others, have faith that there is a Spirit in them, a Spirit that is God, a Spirit that will not fail. The way in which God guides others may be different from the way in which you think they should go. But if you are praying in faith, if you are trusting the power of God, you are able to let go of what you personally think should be the outcome, the answer. You are willing to let God's will be done, for you know that God's will is good, perfect, and true.

Chapter 24

Can We Really Help Others Through Prayer?

All of us try in many ways to help others, especially those near and dear to us. But the greatest help we can give is through prayer, for prayer does what we find impossible to do. Prayer opens the way for God's power to work. Prayer lifts us and the one for whom we pray out of human limitations into the boundless perfection of God.

When we feel that we have failed in our prayers for another, the feeling is usually due to the fact that our prayers have not been answered the way we thought they should be. In praying for others, there is always the temptation to pray for a specific outcome. If I am a mother, concerned about a child who seems to be heading into trouble and difficulty, my prayer may be based more on fear than on faith. I may, in effect, be telling God what it is I want my child to do, the way I want him to act, the direction I want his life to take. When I see no change, I am distressed and shaken in faith; I wonder why God has not answered my prayer.

In praying for others, we really need to pray first for ourselves, to pray for light and peace and understanding. Then we shall be able to let go of anxiety, worry, and fear concerning our dear ones and pray for them with understanding and complete trust. No matter how things may look to us, our prayer reaches past the appearance and affirms our faith in God who is present in the one for whom we pray.

It may seem to us that we can see clearly what is best for others, and it may well be that our vision is right and true. Still, what we want for others and what God is able to do through them are not necessarily the same. As much as we long for the best for our dear ones, our desire cannot compare with the infinite possibilities for good that are in them, that God is ready and willing to unfold through them. When we pray, we help encourage and quicken the Spirit that is in them; we help call forth the God Self. We are never disappointed in our prayers for others when we do not limit them to what we think is right and best, to what we think we should pray for, but enlarge them to encompass the limitless good of God.

What we are also tempted to do when we pray for others is to analyze them, to think that they must act differently before God can bless them or heal them, to feel that they cannot be helped unless they understand Truth as we understand it. This is a subtle temptation; and we are often unaware that even as we attempt to pray for others, we are in our minds criticizing them and seeing their faults and flaws.

When we read the accounts of the healings that Jesus performed, of His prayers for others, we do not find Him saying to anyone, "You are not a good enough person to be healed." He saw the spiritual Self, the God-created person, and His prayer of faith, His spoken word, carried authority and power because He believed in what He saw. The limitations of the personal self cannot defeat the power of God. As we let the power of God flow through us, as we let the light of God shine in us, the limitations drop away, and our prayers become truly effective.

The words *I behold the Christ in you* are good to remember and hold in our prayers for others, for the most effective prayer we can make on anyone's behalf is to behold the Christ in her, the perfect Spirit, the perfect power, the perfect mind, the perfect life, the perfect guide, the perfect peace. Rather than praying, "O God, heal my child," pray in the faith that the healing power of God is already doing its perfect work. Behold the Christ, the life of God, filling your child, flowing through her, healing, renewing, restoring. Every time you think of your child give thanks that she is filled with life, the life of God.

When you are praying for someone who seems to need help desperately, you are not praying to tell God how desperate the need is; rather, you are praying that the one who needs help may become aware of the powerful Spirit of God within, the life-giving, miracle-working power that does not fail. Do not limit God in your prayers for yourself or anyone else, but open the way for God to work freely from within.

When we pray for others, we not only help and bless them but we ourselves are benefited. The more we use our faith, the stronger it becomes. The more we stand firm in Truth, the more we are aware of the goodness of God flowing into our lives, flowing into the lives of those for whom we pray.

There is power in prayer; there is much that we can give to others through our prayers. The greatest gift we can ever give to anyone, the most helpful thing we can ever do for another, is to trust the power of God in that person, to have faith that with this power all things are possible, all disease is curable, all conditions are capable of transformation.

Part V

How to Make a
New Beginning

Chapter 25

This Is the Time for Faith

Is this a time of fear for you? This then is the time for faith! There is never a time when you are alone or helpless, for always God is with you, always divine love surrounds and protects you, always divine Spirit rises in you to give you courage, to keep you steady and calm, to help you overcome fear.

In Psalm 56:3, we read:

> "When I am afraid,
> I put my trust in you."

Resolutely turn away from thoughts of fear to thoughts of faith. Say to yourself: "God is with me, there is nothing to fear. I have put my trust in God. God's perfect love casts out all fear." You can transform a time of fear into a time of faith, a time in which you experience as never before the presence and power of God with you to make you strong and secure.

Is this a time of illness for you? This then is the time for faith! It is the time for remembering that your body is the temple of the living God, that the cells of your body are imbued with living substance, that the healing power of God is mighty in the midst of you. Jesus said that if we have faith as a grain of mustard seed we can move mountains. He said also that with "God all things are possible" (Mt. 19:26). You have faith, more faith than you realize. When you proclaim your faith in God as life, you feel the strength of this faith, for the faith in you is God-inspired and grows and expands as you express it and use it.

So, in the face of illness or disease, proclaim your faith. Bless your body in the realization that every cell is alight and aglow with healing life. Declare your faith in the one life, God-life, in the one power, God-power. Declare your faith in the renewing, rebuilding, restoring process of life that is now perfecting and healing you in every part.

Is this a time of lack for you? It is also a time for faith! It is a time for you to prove your faith in God as supply, it is a time for you to prove the promises of God in spite of appearances or conditions. Every time of doubting God is also a time of proving God. Now is the time for you to rise in faith and remember the promise, "Put me to the test ... see if I will not open the windows of heaven for you and pour down for you an overflowing blessing" (Mal. 3:10).

Now is the time for you to hold to your faith in God as the Source of all, as the Supplier of all good. Now is the time for you to realize and know that your good comes to you from God, that always you have within you rich resources to draw upon and use. Now is the time to establish yourself firmly in the faith that God is with you, that Spirit works through you to bring forth good, that divine love expresses itself through you as the perfect fulfillment of your every need and desire.

Is this a time of grief for you? Then it is also a time for faith! Even in the darkness the light shines, even in the midst of grief the joy of God comes forth to comfort and to bring newness to the heart and mind. A time of grief becomes transformed into a time of joy as we look beyond the shadows, beyond the darkness to the eternal God, to the eternal Truth.

As we look to God, divine love fills us and makes us aware of the real meaning of life. We realize that in God there is only eternal life, that what seem to be endings are beginnings in the eternal plan. We realize, too, as we look with eyes of faith and listen with hearts of faith, that though there may be change, there is no loss or separation. Love keeps us eternally one with those we love. Love transcends grief and binds us in the unity of Spirit in God.

Is this a time of doubt? Then it is also the time for faith! Every occasion to doubt God is an opportunity to prove God. We can even bless our doubts, for it is through lifting our doubting hearts and minds to God that we see. "In your light we see light" (Ps. 36:9). God is proved to us, God's power is proved to us, not by theory or argument, but through faith. As we take our stand for God, as we say to ourselves, to God, "I believe; help my unbelief!" (Mk. 9:24) we find answers and help coming to us in many ways. It is as if God were saying to us: "Do you doubt Me? Only have faith and believe, for here I am in the midst of you. In Me, you live and move and have your being; in Me, is your answer."

Now is the time to have faith, now is the time to discover how great is God's power, how marvelous are God's works, how available is God's presence, how all-encompassing is God's love.

If there is a need of any kind in your life, this is the time for faith! It is the time to find God. And in finding God, you find that this is a blessed time in your life, a time to remember always and forever with thankfulness.

Chapter 26

It Is Never Too Late

"If only I had it to do over again," a person will say, "but it's too late now." And with these words, "It's too late now," he concedes defeat.

How often we feel that nothing can be done about some situation because the time when it could have been met or should have been met, has passed.

In God, there is no time; with God, it is never too late.

Surely there is never a time when prayer is needed more than when we feel most defeated, when it seems that all is lost, when we are faced with the hard, the hopeless, the impossible. The Unity work began because two persons, Charles and Myrtle Fillmore, refused to believe that it was too late. They were middle-aged, struggling financially, both in poor health. Myrtle had been given only six months to live. But they prayed, and they believed and acted on the Truth that God revealed to them. Miracles of healing took place in them because they stood their ground, because they took God at His word, because they followed Jesus Christ in the way of life and light, because they would not, could not be convinced that it was too late.

It is never too late to pray. No matter what the need, condition, or problem, it is never too late for God's power to act, for God's perfect work to be done in mind, body, and affairs. Do not let yourself believe that there is ever a time when God cannot help you.

Jesus, in the healings He performed, never questioned the power of God to heal. He said, "For God all things are possible" (Mt. 19:26). He knew that it was not too late to heal the blind man; it was not too late to heal the man who had been crippled for thirty-eight years; it was not too late to heal the ruler's daughter who had been given up as dead by her family and friends. He spoke the word of life. He knew that where there was faith, there was answered prayer.

If you have need of healing, if you are praying for the healing of someone else, have faith that it is not too late to be healed, that it is never too late for the miracle-working power of God.

Those who condemn themselves for past actions or failures need to know that it is never too late to be forgiven, to be set free. It is never too late to let go of old ways and begin again. If Paul had thought that it was too late for him to change, Christianity would not have had one of its greatest advocates. He said, "Forgetting what lies behind ... I press on toward the goal for the prize of the heavenly call of God in Christ Jesus" (Phil. 3:13-14). We too can forget the things that are behind us. We can begin where we are to live in Christ and experience newness of life.

We too can press forward in faith. We too can make a great and living contribution to the world. It is never too late to begin. What has gone before—age, fears, doubts, or self-condemnation—none of these things can deter or dismay us when we live and act on faith.

The old saying that opportunity knocks only once has been disproved again and again by persons who have risen to make a new life, a new start. The opportunity that passed them by or that they passed by was not the only one. There are always undreamed-of opportunities before us. There are always new paths and new doors opening before us. Rather than sitting back and thinking, "It is too late for me now; it is too late for my life to change; it is too late for me to be the successful person I dreamed of being," say to yourself: "It is never too late for God. There is always a way, there is always the power in me to begin again."

It is never too late to pray; it is never too late to be healed; it is never too late to be forgiven; it is never too late to be successful; it is never too late to find happiness; it is never too late to begin again.

Chapter 27

You Will Forget Your Misery

Have you ever heard a person say, "I could write a book about all the troubles and sorrows I've had"?

The fact is that if this person were to try to write such a book, she might find it most difficult to make her sorrows or troubles seem as real and as terrible as she has imagined them to be. She might even find it difficult to remember the miserable times at all!

Emerson says: "When the act of reflection takes place in the mind, when we look at ourselves in the light of thought, we discover that our life is embosomed in beauty. Behind us, as we go, all things assume pleasing forms, as clouds do far off. Not only things familiar and stale, but even the tragic and terrible are comely as they take their place in the pictures of memory.... The soul will not know either deformity or pain. If in the hours of clear reason we should speak the severest truth, we should say that we had never made a sacrifice.... Neither vexations nor calamities abate our trust. No man ever stated his griefs as lightly as he might."

As we look back, not only do the griefs, the troubles, the unhappinesses become as nothing and take their place in the flowing stream that is our lives; but the same thing is true as we view our present experiences in the light of Truth, from the spiritual viewpoint. This is really what we do when we pray: we lift our thoughts; we reflect on ourselves and our lives; we come into God's presence and see ourselves and all that concerns us as God sees us. This is the power of affirmation: to lift us out of negative, depressing thinking into the powerful light of Truth.

There is a Spirit in you that is one with God. It cannot be hurt, sick, or afraid. It remains untouched by negative experiences.

Even though you may not have been aware of this Spirit, still something in you has always known that you were eternal, immortal, indestructible. Something in you has always known that you were more than you seemed to be, that the person whom family, friends, and acquaintances know as you is not the whole picture, the whole story, not the real Self of you. Even though you may have had only intimations of this God Self in you, only moments of insight, flashes of light when you knew and understood that you are more than flesh and blood, that you are spiritual, that you are a part of God, still these rare moments sufficed to keep your heart happy in its secret knowledge.

Even the person who talks about his troubles, his griefs, his trials, always tries to show us how he has endured. Even to want to do this is the prompting of the soul in him that will not admit defeat.

Sometimes religion is thought to be something that makes us more aware of our sins, more obedient to punishment, more cringing in our attitudes. How far from true this is to anyone who seeks to know God, who follows the light and teachings of Jesus Christ! To come into the knowledge of God, to find the presence of God through prayer, is to find an awareness not of how bad we are but of how good, how wonderful we are as children of God, as children of light. The old ways, the old sins drop away because we see ourselves as we truly are. We are set free through the forgiving love of God to go forward in joy.

When you come into the presence of God, when you are lifted in thought and prayer to a new realization of yourself as a spiritual being, how can you cower, how can you cringe! You stand straight and tall and shining. Now you know yourself as you have always been known by God.

How are those who realize their oneness with God described in the Bible? As shining! As glorious! Say these words out loud. Say them about yourself: *I am shining! I am glorious!* How do they make you feel? You are right to feel uplifted and filled with wonder and awe, to have a sense of the immortality, the indestructibility of life, to feel yourself a part of all this, for indeed you are. You are one with God, you have Christ in you, the hope of glory.

Think about the following words as having meaning for you, as applying to you:

> "Arise, shine; for your light has come,
> and the glory of the Lord has risen
> upon you."
> —Isaiah 60:1

"You will forget your misery;
   you will remember it as waters
      that have passed away.
And your life will be brighter than
      the noonday;
   its darkness will be like the morning."
                                    —Job 11:16-17

The light of God is shining in you, through you, and for you, changing everything from darkness to light. As you stand in the light of God, you see yourself and your life—past, present, and future—as part of the eternal good.

You forget your misery, you remember it only as waters that are passed away. Your life is clearer than the noonday, and what was once darkness is now as the morning.

Chapter 28

How to Make a New Beginning

We all have times when we would like to begin again. Intentionally or unintentionally, we have pursued courses of action that proved unwise; we have caused hurt and unhappiness to ourselves and others. We may feel caught in a vicious circle from which there seems to be no way of escape.

There is always a way out. It is not a way back, not a retracing of our steps in order to find out where we went wrong, but a way forward, a new beginning. It is always possible to begin again. It is never too late to begin again. Any time, in any hour, we can make a new beginning and change our whole lives.

We find that when we decide to make a new beginning, to change our thinking and our ways, the old thoughts, fears, and limitations will try to come back into our minds. We may wonder what we are to do about the conditions that seem so real and that are still facing us, even though we have decided to make a new beginning. We desire to change, but what about the people around us who still see us in the same old way, who seem to deflate us and discourage us in our efforts to be different? And what about our own thoughts that (even more than other persons) keep reminding us of our faults and failures, keep pulling us back to old beliefs and limitations? This is a familiar experience to anyone who has made a fresh start, a new beginning, and it is a challenging experience, of course. But if we stand firm in faith, if we hold to our course with faith and courage, we will emerge victorious and free.

Like unruly children, our thoughts clamor for attention, trying to be heard. Just as a firm, gentle discipline is needed in the rearing of children, so it is needed in the training of our thoughts. Some persons, when they are introduced to the idea of denial, think they have to grit their teeth and deny evil with all their might. But a gentle, disciplined word of denial is a thousand times more effective.

Did Jesus need to shout to the winds and the waves? A firm "Peace! Be still!" was all that was needed to still the elements. So with us: when our thoughts and feelings are turbulent and stormy, we need only to keep poised, to say firmly and faithfully, "Peace! Be still!" and we shall feel a quiet, dynamic power flowing in and through us.

When the old self wants to try to take over, when we find ourselves beginning to think or act in old and unwise ways, then we need to deny the power of the past, to deny the existence in Truth of negation and fear, to declare with confidence that the old thoughts and old conditions are as waters that have passed away. They are no more; they have no power in us or over us or our lives.

Denial should always be followed by affirmation. If we are going to say *no* to something, it is because we are saying *yes* to something else. So when we deny the power of old thoughts and conditions, then we affirm that there is only one Presence and one Power in us, the power of God, the power of Truth, the power of the Christ in us, the God-created perfect Self.

Chapter 29

All Things Work Together for Good

When you have prayed and followed what seemed to you to be the right course of action and things have not worked out, you may be tempted to be discouraged, to doubt, and to question the power of prayer.

It is easy to stand fast in faith when everything is going the way you think it should. It is easy to hold to your vision of good when everything in your world seems right and happy.

And, surprisingly enough, it is easy to maintain this same stand even when everything seems to be working contrary to your desires and plans. It is easy if you refuse to listen to the doubting human self, if you bypass the temptation to give in to negative thinking.

"My brothers and sisters, whenever you face trials of any kind, consider it nothing but joy, because you know that the testing of your faith produces endurance; and let endurance have its full effect, so that you may be mature and complete, lacking in nothing" (Jas. 1:2-4).

"Consider it nothing but joy." Even in the midst of difficulties, we feel a surge of joy as we stand with God and declare our faith. We know that even though we may not be able to see how change will happen, God is with us. God's good is sure and unfailing, and this good is being brought forth.

When we have problems, it is important that we look past them to the Truth, that we see through them to the underlying perfection of Spirit. It is just as important that we see our problems through, that is, that we persist in our faith and in our efforts until the good emerges, as it surely will. See through it; see it through—two ways to meet and overcome any problem.

A favorite Bible text is: "All things work together for good for those who love God" (Rom. 8:28). It is reassuring to know this, to believe this. It changes our view of things; it keeps us from discouragement. It helps us rise above disappointment when things do not work out as we think they should. We can learn to give thanks even for the delays or disappointments. We can learn to see God in them, to have the faith that God's will for us is something higher and better than we have anticipated or planned.

"All things work together for good." This indicates a "working-together" time. This time, if we do not understand it, may seem to be a time of frustration and delay, but if we understand what is happening, we see that when we invoke the power of God in our lives, when we commit ourselves to God's good purposes, we then experience all things working together for good. Yeast needs time to work in the dough to rise; the seed needs time to germinate in the ground to grow. We can learn to let patience have its perfect work in us to be perfect and entire, lacking nothing.

"Consider it nothing but joy." This is the way of sure growth and unfoldment, to count every experience as good, as part of the process by which we are coming into light and understanding. This is the sure way to rise out of disappointment, to let go of our preconceived ideas of how things should work out in our lives or in the lives of others, to let go of our human ideas of what our good or the good of another may be, to trust utterly in God, to desire only God's good.

Sometimes we will want and hope for good, but we do not see that we have a part in the outworking. With every thought and feeling, with every word we contribute to the working out process, we hasten the coming of the good of God in our lives.

Do we work with all things as if we had faith in the underlying good? Do we see the good in the situations that arise daily, do we see God in our homes, in our families, in our acquaintances? Do we see the good in spite of appearances, when there seems to be injustice, when someone seems to be undermining our best interests? "Consider it nothing but joy." These are the times when we prove our faith, our patience, our trust, when we prove the nothingness of error, the reality of good.

When things are not going the way you had

hoped, when your prayers do not seem to be answered, do not let yourself become discouraged. Let the working-together process continue. Hold fast to your faith in the good. In ways that you cannot now see or even imagine, all things are working together for good.

God is with you, and God's ways are wondrous. God will never leave you or forsake you, but will always fulfill His good will and purpose through you.

Chapter 30

This Is the Day

If you had only one day of life, you would try to make that one day count. It would be a day when every moment had meaning, a day when everything and everyone mattered.

In a sense all we ever have is one day: today. Yesterday is gone, tomorrow is yet to be, but right now, this day, at this moment in time, we live.

To learn to live one day at a time, to learn to live in the present, the now, is something that most of us need to do. Sometimes our days seem so crowded, there is so much carried over from yesterday, so much facing us tomorrow, that we lose the sense of the present. We let the joy of today, the here and now, pass us by.

If you will begin your day with these words from the Psalms it will help you to set the pattern of your day: "This is the day that the Lord has made; let us rejoice and be glad in it" (Ps. 118:24).

How will you rejoice and be glad in this day?

Pray today. Let this be a day when a prayer of thankfulness sings in your heart, when a prayer of faith fills your mind, a day of prayer without ceasing. Driving a car, making a bed, answering mail, working with the public—whatever you are doing, you

can do it with a sense of God's presence and power
with you, you can do it with a feeling that God is at
work. Divine love is all-pervading, God's presence is
all-sustaining. Pray today, not just in words, not just
at set times, but with every thought, with every
breath let God be praised.

Work today. Work with a sense of ease and joy, a
sense of light and freedom. Work as though there is
only today. The burdens and cares of the past are
gone. You do not need to worry about tomorrow or
next week or next year. You need only give your
thought, your time, your interest, your attention to
the things in hand. What is before you today? Work
today, accomplish today, for God is with you, working
through you, giving you the strength, the energy, the
will to do all that you need to do today.

Give today. As you give, you will know the true joy
of living. You may wonder what you have to give, but
as you pray, "God, let me be a channel through
which Your good is given," as you are ready and willing to give of yourself, you will see ways and means
and opportunities for giving. Giving may be a giving
of material help; more often it is a giving of spiritual
qualities. It is the giving of encouragement, the giving of faith, appreciation, love, understanding. Give
something to someone today. It will add meaning
and joy to your day.

Grow today. This is the day to do more than
merely exist; it is the day to expand, to grow. Jesus
likened the kingdom of heaven to a mustard seed,
symbolic of growth and expansion. Grow today in
the kingdom-of-heaven idea. Rather than thinking of
the kingdom of heaven as something vague or as

something to look forward to after death, remember that Jesus said that the kingdom of God is within you. The way of growth, the way of unfoldment is to realize that God is within you, that God's expanding, unfolding kingdom is within you. This is the day to grow in Truth.

This is the day to realize that right now you live in the kingdom of heaven, right now you are the beloved child of God, right now you have a wonderful Spirit within you.

Live today. Live in the fullest sense of the word. Do not be content with feeling half alive. Call the cells of your body to life. Let the sleeping cells of mind and body come alive in Christ. Declare the life of Christ in you. You are alive in Christ: Christ is alive in you. Feel the call to life of the living Christ in you, and rise in health and strength and radiant wholeness. Live today!

Chapter 31

Not Someday, but Now

"The present is the point at which time touches eternity."

If you are hoping and praying that someday you will be healed, someday you will be successful, someday you will be happy, change this hope, this prayer, from someday to now.

Right now you are living in eternity, right now you are a child of God, right now you are one with your good.

Do not ask, "When shall I be healed?" Right now you are in the midst of life; right now God's healing power is mightily at work in you. Do not limit God's power by thinking that it cannot come now. Do not deny God by thinking that some condition is beyond help, that some healing need is too hard for God. All the healing life there is, is present with you and in you, right now. You are alive in God. The cells of your body are the creation of God. The healing power is present where you are. God is your healer in this present moment.

Do you dream of the time when your ship will

come in, when you will be prosperous and success-ful? Right now you live in the midst of plenty. The supply of God will be no greater at any future time than it is now. Your good is always at hand. Why post-pone receiving it; why dream of it instead of claim-ing it? The substance of God lies all about you; the riches of God fill the universe to overflowing. The goodness of God is freely given. God says to you, "Put me to the test ... see if I will not open the win-dows of heaven for you and pour down for you an overflowing blessing" (Mal. 3:10). What is your need, what do you long for? Prove God now by trusting God and by knowing that supply for every need is already waiting for you.

Do you long for some heavenly time when all will be peaceful and serene? God's peace is here now. God's peace has never left you. God's peace is with you always. You do not have to wait until conditions in your life are perfect in order to experience peace. The peace of God surrounds you, fills you, perme-ates you now. You do not have to wait for others to change in order to experience harmony. Serenity of spirit, harmony of mind and soul are yours now. They are part of your God nature.

What of wisdom, what of love, what of joy, what of light? Are you experiencing them now? You should be, for right now God is blessing you.

Where shall you search for wisdom? Where is the answer, the guidance you pray for? "Be still, and know that I am God!" (Ps. 46:10) The all-knowing Mind of God is in you. In this Mind is pure wisdom, from this Mind comes divine guidance. In commu-nion with Divine Mind, you find the answers to your questions, the end of all your seeking. "When you search for me, you will find me; if you seek me with all your heart" (Jer. 29:13).

What has gone before cannot take away your joy. No bitterness or resentment or unforgivingness can remain in your heart or life as you live in the presence of God. "You show me the path of life. In your presence there is fullness of joy" (Ps. 16:11).

The love of God sweeps away depression or fear and fills you with strength and faith. It lifts you out of old ways of thinking or reacting. You see that you do not have to seek love or try to win the love or affection of others. You are one with the love of God and in this oneness you are united with other people.

Right now God is blessing you. Can you believe this? Whatever your need may be, will you take this stand, make this affirmation of Truth and life for yourself? If your need is for healing, hold the thought that right now God is healing you. If you are having trouble getting along with someone, affirm that right now God is blessing the situation. If your pocketbook seems empty, deny the appearance and know that right now the substance of God fills your life.

Right now you have faith, faith that is God-given, faith that is not dependent on your capacity to receive but is as large, as boundless as God's capacity to give.

Right now you are in the presence of God. Nothing else is needed. You have all, for you have God.

Chapter 32

You Were Born to Be Rich

None of us hesitates to think in terms of perfect health, none of us hesitates to pray for healing; but some of us do not feel that we have a right to think in terms of riches and success. We hesitate to pray for anything as materialistic as prosperity.

But, as Emerson says, "Man was born to be rich, or inevitably grows rich by the use of his faculties."

You were born to be rich, whatever the circumstances of your environment. You came into the world possessed of the powers and faculties that create richness and success.

Too many people allow themselves to go along in life feeling impoverished. They blame circumstances, they blame lack of opportunity; they feel that they have no possible chance of ever becoming prosperous. As they think, so they are. And prosperity and success are barred to those who think in terms of lack, who are too timid to think richly.

We think of good fortune as coming to us—an unexpected inheritance, money dropped in our laps from heaven—but good fortune comes through us, not to us. We are our own good fortune; we have within us powers and capabilities that, if used, would create a whole new world for us, a rich, prosperous, successful world. There is an old saying that every child comes into the world with a loaf of bread in his mouth. This is another way of saying that we come into the world divinely blessed with all that we need.

Every person has something unique to contribute to the world. She is needed, and no one else can quite give what she has to give. We need to remember this, that we are unique individuals, that we have been endowed with talents and powers and capabilities that need to be expressed by us and through us. When we pray for prosperity, invariably we are stirred to new incentive. We are quickened to a new understanding of what we can do to bring forth more supply in our lives. We are inspired with rich ideas, and we are filled with the will and the strength to act on these ideas.

Another thing that invariably happens when we pray for prosperity is that we look at ourselves and our lives from a new standpoint; we see how rich we already are. We look with appreciation on all our blessings; our hearts are filled with thankfulness for the good that surrounds us, the beauty in which we walk and live, the richness of love and joy that are a part of our everyday lives.

Prosperity is to a great extent a state of mind. How we feel about ourselves, our abilities, our ends, our goals, our purposes makes us either rich in spirit or impoverished in consciousness.

We can change our thinking, we can have a new perception of ourselves. We can remind ourselves that we were born to be rich, that we have within us the capacity for successful, prosperous living.

The source of our supply is the one Source. Just as our health, our strength, our peace of mind come from within, from the living presence of God, so the outer supply that seems so solid and material has its source within, has its beginning in God, and is brought forth and made manifest through the application of mind to spiritual ideas.

To all appearances, many people have set incomes; they plan and budget to cover the essentials. They have a feeling of "this much and no more." But the substance of God is unlimited, and this substance is that from which we draw our good. Our supply is limited only because we set limits in our minds. We let ourselves fall into circumscribed ways of thinking and living. We do not think in terms of increase or enrichment but rather in terms of getting by, or barely meeting our needs.

We may say: "But where is the supply to come from? How can my good be increased?" The supply of Spirit, the riches of the kingdom, come *through us, not to us.* This is one of the most important truths that we need to realize. The way of increase and enrichment is through expanding our consciousness of God as provider, through expanding our consciousness of ourselves as inheritors of the kingdom. This expansion does not come by just wishing for it. It comes through prayer, through the enlarging and increasing of our awareness of the power of God within us, through the awareness of our oneness with our source, our oneness with supply.

Chapter 33

How to Release Your Power

Anyone who has ever prayed earnestly and sincerely for prosperity has discovered that the answer came, not as manna falling from heaven, but as an idea that cried out for action. We are always a part of the answer to our prayers, for the answer is the activity of God, and this activity takes place through us. When we pray, we open ourselves to the power of God that is within us. This power has been there all the time, and as it is released, we are stirred to action.

Sometimes our greatest need, if we lack prosperity, is not in the outer at all. Our need is an inner need, a need to release our tremendous power to achieve. We look at others and perhaps envy them their energy, their drive, their zest. We think that it is no wonder they are successful and prosperous.

But the matter of energy is rather paradoxical. We do not necessarily conserve energy by resting, by sparing ourselves, by making halfhearted efforts to do what needs to be done. The less energy we use, the less we seem to have. Energy used creates more energy.

Where do we make a start in stirring up energy? First of all we need to pray, to affirm our oneness with the presence of God, with the Source of all power, the Source of our strength. But let us pray in faith believing; let us pray with interest, enthusiasm, and expectation. Enthusiasm is an energy sparker, not only physically but spiritually. Enthusiasm adds to the effectiveness of our prayers. Louis Pasteur once called *enthusiasm* "the inner God." When we are enthusiastic, when we are filled with the desire to know and to express God, a divine activity takes place in us and in our lives. Just as atomic energy is released through a chain reaction, so spiritual energy is released in us. One positive affirmation of Truth can release tremendous forces for good in us.

When you use affirmations, think of them as energy releasers, think of them as power producers, think of them as stirring up God-activity. To think of affirmations in this way will give new impetus to the words of Truth you speak, will give greater reinforcement to your faith.

In Isaiah we read, "He gives power to the faint, and strengthens the powerless.... But those who wait for the Lord shall renew their strength, they shall mount up with wings like eagles, they shall run and not be weary, they shall walk and not faint" (Is. 40:29, 31). Here are the two parts to successful prayer, to successful living: first the waiting, then the acting. We wait upon the Lord when we spend time in the silence; when we commune with God in our souls; when we open ourselves to the living Presence, to the all-knowing Spirit. Then we mount up with "wings like eagles," that is, we rise with new faith to meet our problems, with a new heart to understand, with a new will to overcome, with a new enthusiasm for living, with a new burst of energy and power. Then we find ourselves part of the God-activity, and our lives are blessed. Our efforts become more purposeful, and our contributions more effective. We not only go to meet our good, we find that our good comes running to meet us from every direction.

This is the secret of successful living, this is the secret of a prosperous life, to wait on the Lord, that is, to take the time to feel our oneness with Spirit, to let it fill us, infuse us with life so that we meet each day, each experience with confidence, filled with living enthusiasm.

Part VI

Your Transcendent Spirit

Chapter 34

There Is Freedom for You

Have you ever thought that when you want freedom from something, it is because you want freedom to do or to be something else?

A person who is fearful of many things, for instance, wants freedom from fear so that he can meet the experiences of life with courage. He does not want just freedom from fear. He wants, above all, strength of spirit and the courage to fearlessly face whatever or whoever has intimidated him. He wants freedom from fear so that he can live courageously and effectively.

Those who are filled with feelings of guilt and remorse over the past want freedom from these feelings; but more than this they want to be able to accept the forgiving love of Jesus Christ, to let the past go. They are bound not by a sense of guilt or regret or remorse as much as by an inability to forget, to forgive, and to accept the forgiveness that is always a part of God's love. They want freedom from thoughts of the past so that they may experience a new awareness of the present. It is not freedom from the past that is needed, but freedom to go forward, confidently sure of God's love, sure of their worth as beloved children of God.

Sometimes we are in bondage to negative thinking without realizing it. In fact, we may feel justified in our feelings, even to a degree proud of them. We have all known persons who carried resentments and hurt feelings along with them for years. Someone treated them badly, betrayed their trust, or cheated them out of money, and the resentment remains. A mere mention of the offender's name will bring all the memories back, and the resentment, the righteous indignation will rise to the surface again. But anyone who is filled with resentment toward anyone or anything, no matter how justified the resentment may seem to be, is not free, but bound in limited, self-defeating thinking.

Perhaps the greatest bondage we feel is to a place or person. We may find ourselves in a job that we dislike, but we do not feel free to make a change. We are not sure that we could better the situation, so we go along wearily from day to day, feeling trapped and unhappy. What we need is not freedom from a dull or boring job but the freedom to hold new thoughts about ourselves, about our worth, about the importance of everything we do. When we work with a sense of freedom and joy, it hardly matters what we do, for we work with a sense of accomplishment; and we know that every little bit somehow contributes to the whole.

Often a person will feel in great bondage to some other person. Often she truly loves the other person, but at the same time feels that she is not free to live her own life because of the responsibility for this person's care that rests upon her. She sees no way out of bondage. She can only envision herself as going along in the same way, subordinating her hopes and desires to the will or even the whim of another. She does not need freedom from bondage to another person as much as she needs freedom to know and recognize herself as a spiritual being and to rise out of old limited thoughts about herself. She needs the freedom to realize that no one else has bound her, or can ever bind her, and that her bondage has been in her own thoughts. Her freedom comes through a change of thought, a change of consciousness.

Too often we think that if only we were in a different place, in a different set of circumstances with different people, we would be happy and free. We postpone our freedom, thinking that someday we will not be tied down, someday we will not be afraid to act, someday people will treat us differently and will respect us and recognize our worth. But the someday we are waiting for is already here. Now is the time for freedom, now "we are children of God." Freedom is of the Spirit and cannot be restricted by anything outside ourselves, nor can it be given to us by anything or anyone outside ourselves. Freedom is the result of realizing our oneness with God, of rising in thought and consciousness until we see ourselves as we truly are, spiritual beings, forever and eternally free, living in a spiritual world, governed by spiritual ideas. A lifting thought such as, *I am not bound in personal consciousness, I am free with the freedom of Spirit,* will lift us out of anything in our own thinking that has limited us. In Spirit, we are free.

Chapter 35

Your Transcendent Spirit

Have you ever had the experience of having a problem disappear as soon as you were able to lift your thought about it? There is that in you which is greater than any need or problem, which transcends every human limitation. This all-powerful, all-healing presence is the Christ in you.

You need not go along struggling and striving with conditions that seem beyond you. You need not feel defeated by disease, lack, or limiting circumstances. You are Spirit! This is what makes the difference; this is the source of your power; this is the assurance of your success.

You may have grown accustomed to thinking of yourself as just an ordinary human being, with no special talents or abilities. You may have accepted the thought that you are bound to an unhappy or unproductive way of life. You may have gone along with the belief that it is not your right to have a full and free life, that you are unworthy or undeserving. But such a negative outlook on life can be changed;

it is changed, once you begin to think of yourself in terms of spiritual reality. Even more quickly than your mind has accepted negative beliefs, it will respond and accept true ideas—God ideas. And an idea of Truth is powerful and transforming; it goes to work at once to change your whole thought, your whole life.

Most people believe in prayer. They turn to God, seeking help and guidance; but to them God may remain far off until they rise in thought to the place where they know that they are one with God, that they are not praying to something outside themselves but are merging the human with the divine, calling forth the God presence.

The strain of daily life may be so great, the demands on your thought and time and energy so consuming, that you feel unequal to them and do not know what to do about them. You may intuitively feel that you are only expressing half of what you are capable of expressing.

Often a basic idea of Truth will do a powerful job of changing the direction of your thinking and living, of elevating your consciousness. One such idea is, *I transcend myself and all my concerns, for I am Spirit.* Say these words over to yourself; let them sink into your mind; make them a vital approach to everything you do.

Are you trying to make a decision and finding it difficult? Say to yourself: *I transcend myself and all my concerns, for I am Spirit.* Where before you have been trying to think things through, reason things out, now let go. Know that you are Spirit, that you have the Christ Mind in you, that you are in touch, in tune with perfect spiritual ideas. Whatever you need to know will be revealed. The transcendent power of Spirit in you pours light upon your path and reveals ways where before there seemed to be no way.

If you feel burdened by any condition or situation, take this freeing idea and let it lift you out of bondage: *I transcend myself and all my concerns, for I am Spirit.*

You have great inner resources, for you are spiritually created. You have God's own Spirit within you. You have been created with capabilities and powers that you have barely begun to express.

This transcendent idea is not one to be reserved for big events, for moments of great need or great decisions. It is an idea to keep in mind every day, to hold to as you meet and handle the things that may not seem of importance to anyone else but are important to you. The minor things that are annoying or irritating need to be transcended as much as, or perhaps more than, the major ones, for often we are worn down, depressed by something that is petty in itself but has been magnified out of proportion in our minds. If you find yourself frustrated or perplexed in even small matters, do not let yourself stay down. You are Spirit! Remember this. Remind yourself again and again: *I transcend myself and all my concerns, for I am Spirit.*

Power is in you waiting to be used; life is in you waiting to be called forth; love is in you waiting to be expressed; joy is in you waiting to overflow. You are a wonderful, remarkable, unique creation. You are Spirit!

Chapter 36

Have You Ever Heard God's Voice?

Have you ever heard God's voice? Of course you have! Every time you have had faith, every time you have expressed love, every time you have felt joy, you have heard God. God's voice, God's word, is God expressing through you; it is Spirit moving in and through you; it is God's power working mightily in you. To hear God, to be aware of God is to be conscious of God's presence.

Sometimes people think they are not divinely guided because they do not hear a voice out of heaven telling them what to do. They are looking for external signs and wonders. But this is not the way God's word comes; it comes as a still, small voice, a voice that we hear in the silence. God's word comes to us in thoughts, in ideas, in feelings; God's word comes as spiritual quickening, as an inflow of faith, as a realization of peace.

Because we do not realize that this is the way God speaks to us, we may reject the spiritual ideas that come to us as worthless, because we ourselves have thought of them. We look elsewhere for enlightenment. We search and search for someone or some book to reveal the mystery of faith to us, when all the time the key is hidden within our hearts.

We are like the Children of Israel who wanted to find the Promised Land, but who wanted Moses to do all the listening to God for them and do all their praying for them. They wanted him to find out from God what they were supposed to do and then show them how to do it. Moses at Moab said to them, "Surely, this commandment that I am commanding you today is not too hard for you, nor is it too far away. It is not in heaven, that you should say, 'Who will go up to heaven for us, and get it for us so that we may hear it and observe it?' Neither is it beyond the sea, that you should say, 'Who will cross to the other side of the sea for us, and get it for us so that we may hear it and observe it?' No, the word is very near to you; it is in your mouth and in your heart for you to observe" (Deut. 30:11-14).

When we long for guidance in some matter, when we wish that we could hear the word of God as did the prophets of old, let us remember that the word is very near to us, in our mouths, and in our hearts, that we may observe it.

What a difference it makes in the way we pray, in the way we think, in the way we live when we realize that God is in us, that every time we speak a word of Truth we are giving voice to God's word! Our words become alive and powerful as we realize what it means to have God's word in our mouths and in our hearts.

"By faith we understand that the worlds were prepared by the word of God, so that what is seen was made from things that are not visible" (Heb. 11:3). Your world has been framed by the word of God spoken through you, and it is continually being shaped and formed by faith, the faith of God that is in you and is expressed through you.

Whenever you are in need of light or guidance, when you do not know how to handle some situation, when you are troubled about your life or the life of someone else, in the quietness of your inner thought remind yourself: *The word of faith is in my heart. It is not too hard for me, nor is it too far away. It is not in heaven that someone has to go up for me and bring it to me and make me hear it, that I may observe it. Neither is it beyond the sea, that I wonder who will go over the sea for me and bring it to me and make me hear. The word is very near to me, in my mouth, and in my heart, that I may observe it. I hear God's word and follow His instructions.*

When you speak words of faith, words of life, words of strength, words of joy, words of substance, words of wisdom, do you realize that you are speaking God's word? Jesus said that His words were Spirit and life, and your words can be Spirit and life, too, as you let God-ideas express through you.

Watch your words; you may discover that you have been using negative words without realizing it, words that depress or discourage, words that actually deny God's presence and power. God's word is very near to you, in your mouth and in your heart. Your words can become God's words, filled with life, quickened with faith.

Chapter 37

What Do You Expect?

To expect the good, to expect answers to our prayers—this we think of as faith. The other half of expecting is waiting, and we do not often associate waiting with faith. In fact, if we pray with great faith and expectation and our answer does not come immediately, if we have to wait, we may think that we have failed, that our faith has failed. In our despair we may even think that God has failed. "My soul, wait thou only upon God; for my expectation is from him" (Ps. 62:5 KJV).

Expecting and waiting: both are forms of faith. It takes faith to expect answers to prayer, to expect healing in the midst of pain, to expect guidance when darkness envelopes us, to expect peace when turmoil prevails, to expect success though we have previously failed.

First it takes faith to expect answers to prayer; then it takes faith to wait for the results that we believe are forthcoming. The illustration of the planted seed has been cited often, and it is a perfect one. If we plant a seed in the ground, we expect it to grow, we expect to see the shoot, the full-grown plant. We also expect and accept a waiting period. We know that no amount of worry or anxiety will change the pattern—the planted seed must germinate and grow. If we hover over it, if we dig it up to see what is the matter, we know that it cannot survive. We plant in faith; we await the coming forth of that which we have planted with a faith that is no less important.

When Jesus compared faith to a grain of mustard, He was showing us that our expectation can far surpass the present smallness of that in which we place our faith. An acorn is a small seed, but "lo! the mighty oak."

In your own life, in the lives of others you have seen again and again how even a small degree of faith produced great and wondrous results.

When Jesus said that we need to become as little children, surely He referred to the implicit faith of the child, the great expectation with which the child greets every day. The little child accepts each day as it comes, with no feeling of waiting for things to happen, with no backward glances. The child lives joyously in the present.

So we, too, can learn to live with faith, to expect joy and good in every day, to pray and expect large and far-reaching results to our prayer, but still not fret or fume or try to hurry our good. We know that God is all, that God is the perfect fulfillment to all desire, the unfailing answer to every prayer we can make.

When we pray in faith, we follow the pattern of expecting and waiting. We all understand what it is to expect; sometimes we do not realize that to wait means more than to stand still. It is to realize, to know that our expectation is from God. Every time of knowing the Truth, of realizing our oneness with God, of feeling God's presence and power, is a time of waiting, a time in which we let go and let God, a time in which we cease our straining and striving, and stand still and trust.

Our attitude of mind colors everything we do. The attitude in which we expect, in which we wait, makes the difference in the results that come. Sometimes our expectation is not on a high enough level. It is expectation, yes, but the kind that says: "I expect a lot from life. After all, I deserve it. I expect a great deal from my family and friends. Look at all I have done for them." This kind of expectation usually leads to disappointment and frustration. When our expectation comes from persons and circumstances, it may seem to us that life is unjust or unfair, that other persons have let us down, that we have failed to receive that which we deserved.

The attitude in which we wait for answers to prayer, for the flowering of good in our lives, is important. Too many of us think of waiting as wasting time; we think of waiting as something that delays us, thwarts us. When we change this idea to "wait ... only upon God," we rise out of the old way of looking at waiting. We see that waiting can be a blessed time, an active time, a growing time, a time in which we do not stand still. It is a time in which we stand with God, knowing with certainty that God is at work in our lives, knowing with certainty that divine love never fails.

We cannot expect too much of God. We should expect life—glowing, radiant, perfect life in our bodies. We should expect guidance—guidance in all our ways, light on all our paths. We should expect inspiration and revelation. We should expect supply, substance—abundant good to flow into our lives, freely, fully, without limitation.

The greatest expectation of all is the expectation that we have of knowing ourselves as children of God, of finding the living Christ in ourselves, of putting on the Christ nature that is perfect, pure, eternal.

"For the creation waits with eager longing for the revealing of the children of God" (Rom. 8:19).

This is our great expectation, this is what everything in us waits for—to know ourselves and others as we are known, as God knows us, God's beloved, God's own.

Chapter 38

Do Not Magnify Negation: Magnify Good

Fear usually wears magnifying glasses. But so does faith!

When we are afraid, we do not see things in their right proportions; our troubles may seem twice as large as they actually are. Our fear magnifies the appearance of negation and makes us feel helpless before it.

What kind of magnifying glasses does faith wear? Faith says, "My soul magnifies the Lord" (Lk. 1:47). Faith uses the magnification of praise. Faith says, "God is all and God is good; what is there to fear!" Faith needs only the cloud as large as a man's hand to see, as Elijah saw, the promise of showers of blessings.

Sometimes we tend to magnify the negation in our lives more than the good. Hardly anyone becomes dramatic telling about the good things that have happened to him, but there are some persons who are always trying to be in the center of the stage telling everyone who will listen about the terrible things they have had to meet. In order to hold their audience of family or friends, they magnify their troubles, they enlarge on their pain, their suffering, on the hardships they have had to endure, on the injustices they have had to suffer.

To do this sort of thing may invoke the sympathy of others and it may assure a person of a responsive audience, but the small satisfaction that this brings cannot compensate the one person directly and adversely affected by such magnification of negation—the one who is doing the talking!

The trouble is that if we keep talking about our ills and exaggerating them, we are the ones who are impressed the most, we are the ones who feel the full impact of our own words. Other persons may shrug off the tales of woe that are poured into their ears, for they know that most things are not half as bad as they sound; the one doing the telling, however, may begin to believe that everything that has happened to him has been twice as bad as anything that ever happened to anyone else.

It is often a temptation to magnify our fears. When we find ourselves dreading some situation, letting our fearful imaginations run ahead of us and away with us, let us stop this trend of thought and feeling by remembering God, by magnifying God. The Psalmist said: "Say continually, 'Great is the Lord!' " (Ps. 40:16)

This is something that all of us can learn to say continually: *Jehovah be magnified. God be magnified, the good be magnified.* "My soul magnifies the Lord, and my spirit rejoices in God my Savior."

What does it mean to magnify the Lord? It means to make God large in your life, to see and know and feel the Presence and Power so clearly and surely that nothing dismays you, nothing shakes your faith.

God is the only power. Think about this power, magnify it, extol it, praise it.

> "Bless the Lord, O my soul,
>   and all that is within me,
>   bless his holy name.
> Bless the Lord, O my soul,
>   and do not forget all his benefits—
> who forgives all your iniquity,
>   who heals all your diseases,
> who redeems your life from the Pit,
>   who crowns you with steadfast love and
>   mercy,
> who satisfies you with good as long as you
>   live
> so that your youth is renewed like
>   the eagle's."
>   —Psalm 103:1-5

Newspapers, television, radio, magazines often magnify the troubles of the world. Why? Because troubles make news—bad news, to be sure, but news that always finds an interested audience. Each one of us can be our own editor; we can refuse to enlarge on or dwell on all the negative happenings. We can be our own publisher too. "How beautiful upon the mountains are the feet of the messenger who announces peace, who brings good news" (Is. 52:7).

It is good to announce peace, to bring good news to others; it is more important to bring this good news, to announce this peace to our own thoughts, first of all. Here is where you magnify the Lord, here is where you magnify the good, in your inmost self, in your heart, in your mind, in the way you think and feel.

Chapter 39

You Live in God; God Lives in You

The most marvelous idea that you can hold is that you are alive in God. You live in God; God lives in you.

The life you have been praying for is here, in you now. The healing you have been praying for is already accomplished, for you are one with God's healing power, right now. God's healing life is mighty in the midst of you, making you whole.

Have you in your prayers for healing been inclined to think of healing as something to be accomplished at some future time? Have you prayed for strength to bear your present misery and hoped for healing, sometime, somehow?

There is no limitation on God's healing power, no delay, no time involved. Then why are we not healed instantly? The delay, the limitation can only be in us, in our unawareness of our oneness, of our unity with life, eternal, healing life, now in the instant in which we voice a prayer.

If there is God-life in every part of our bodies, then there is God-intelligence too. The body is not

just an unresponsive mass: it is built of Spirit substance; it is the image-and-likeness creation of God.
Most of us do not think of our bodies in this way,
especially when we are not manifesting perfect
health. We are aware of the aches, the pains, the
things that seem wrong, and we burden the body
further by our fears and nagging worries concerning
it.

Myrtle Fillmore wrote once that she had made a
discovery, a discovery that was to transform and heal
her body. This discovery was that intelligence as well
as life is needed to make a body. She said: "Here is
the key to my discovery. Life has to be guided by
intelligence in making all forms. The same law works
in my own body. Life is simply a form of energy, and
has to be guided and directed in man's body by his
intelligence. How do we communicate intelligence?
By thinking and talking, of course. Then it flashed
upon me that I might talk to the life in every part of
my body and have it do just what I wanted. I began
to teach my body and got marvelous results."

This may seem a strange idea to you, and you may
feel a little foolish at first if you are led to follow Mrs.
Fillmore's suggestions. But they point out a key idea,
and a principle that is founded on Truth. The power
of the spoken word has been proved again and
again, but most of us have not thought of actually
talking to the body. We think of it constantly, of
course. We are aware of any unusual response in it.
We talk about how we feel. But we do not talk to the
body itself. It is the overlooked, neglected and often
overworked vehicle that responds to our ideas about
it, that is often burdened and heavy laden because of

our unhappy, fearful, unloving thoughts and feelings.

Like Mrs. Fillmore we can find healing by changing our thoughts about our bodies, by blessing and
praising the life and intelligence in every part.

If there is the appearance of disease or ill health,
do not be dismayed by it, but have faith that the life
of God in you is powerful and perfect, quick to heal,
mighty to restore.

You can praise and bless your way out of every
negative condition of mind or body. So if you find it
difficult at first to quit thinking or talking in terms of
illness or disease, begin to add the idea of blessing
and praising to your thoughts and words. When
there are aches and pains, then is the time to praise
and bless your body even more for the good work
that it is doing, for the life and intelligence that are
in every part.

Do not be discouraged or impatient if the body
does not respond all at once to this new thought
which you are giving it. It has to learn new ways from
you. The important thing to remember is that even
as you pray, even as you speak words of life and
praise, you are one with God. God's life is in you;
God's healing work is being done in you.

Healing is not to be hoped for or dreamed about;
it is a present reality.

There is life and intelligence in every part of your
body; there is a will to live that is strong in you. God
has made you for life. God has given you a marvelous body, "fearfully and wonderfully made." God
within you is the directing power. You can trust God
for healing. You live in God; God lives in you.

Part VII

Every Experience Is Our Teacher

Chapter 40

Why Do We Grieve?

Why do we grieve when someone we love goes through the change called death? Often the reason we grieve is because we reproach ourselves for the things we did not do, the things we left unsaid, or the things that were said that we cannot recall or take back.

Everyone who has lost someone near and dear has had some of these feelings to contend with. Because no human relation measures up to the perfect ideal of love, we feel that we have failed, that somehow, in some way, we could have given more of ourselves, we could have reached out and truly helped another.

The comfort we need is not just the comfort of knowing that our dear one is alive in God and eternally one with God, but that this has always been true.

If we are reproaching ourselves for failure to provide our loved one with something that we thought she lacked, we need to know that God is the one provider, that always God has provided her with whatever she needed. We should not think that her life lacked love because we were not more loving. Always God has been with her as the love that satisfied her soul, even as God is with us. Therefore, we should not reproach ourselves for what we failed to do for another, for it has been and always will be the Spirit in her that works through her to bring her own to her.

When we think about ourselves and our lives, we know our inner needs and desires, we know that no person in the world can truly satisfy them, that only as we live close to God and let Spirit find expression through us do we find happiness, peace, and satisfaction. We would not want someone else to feel remorseful because we are not completely at peace, completely happy, completely successful, would we? We know that our answer does not lie outside ourselves, does not rest with other persons, but with God and us.

It helps us to overcome grief when we realize this; it helps us to release and bless those who pass from one phase of soul experience to another. We see them as children of God, and we keep faith in them as children of God. We are willing to let go of our possessive love for them, our personal desires for them. We are willing to release them into the larger concept of love, love that is of the Spirit.

Another source of grief is our feeling of helplessness without the presence of someone on whom we have come to depend. We think that we cannot go on without him; we think that we shall be unable to live our lives without his help, without his love. It is not easy to face life on our own, but we need to realize that we never have to do this. We are never alone;

we are never on our own. Always we have God's presence with us.

When we feel lost or bereft without someone, let us pray for light, let us pray for a new awareness of the presence of God. Jesus said, "I am with you always, to the end of the age" (Mt. 28:20). The Christ presence is with us always, changeless, abiding. As much as we have loved another person, as much as we have come to depend on him, materially, mentally, emotionally, even spiritually, when he departs from the scene of our world, we are not left defenseless or helpless. We find, as we pray, that we still have the sense of being loved and cared for, for whom we really depended on was God. The love that we relied on was God's love, the support we felt really came from God.

Nothing has changed, really. The absence of our loved one has opened our eyes to a new truth, has made us see with a larger vision, has brought us to a new place in understanding. We see that love remains, that courage remains, that life remains. We see new things in ourselves that we had not been aware of. We discover new capabilities for entering into life that we had not suspected. We uncover new depths of courage and faith that we had not known were there.

Why do we grieve? We do not grieve for long when we pray, when we let God take over our minds, our hearts, our feelings.

> "Weeping may linger for the night,
> but joy comes with the morning."
> —Psalm 30:5

After the first impact of grief, the night of weeping, the light breaks through and joy comes, the joy of knowing that life is eternal, that there is no separation in Spirit, that underneath it all are the everlasting arms of love that support us, strengthen us, and make us know that all is well.

Chapter 41

Every Experience Is Our Teacher

Every one of us has had experiences to meet that at first seemed difficult but proved to be times of growth and gain. Through these experiences, we discovered new strengths in ourselves, we unfolded new powers and capabilities, we experienced a closer unity with God, and we relied on God with a faith greater than we knew we possessed.

Every experience is our teacher; we learn from the persons, the events, the circumstances that surround us. Most of the time we are not aware that we are learning because we are more aware of the struggle we are making. Like the child struggling to get to her feet, to learn to walk, we do not see that our efforts are teaching us and freeing us.

We are being molded and shaped, not by outer circumstances or by other persons but from within, by our reactions, our thoughts, our feelings, our attitudes. And yet, unless we have experiences to meet that make us seek deeper for understanding, reach higher for light, we do not develop our spiritual nature. To realize this truth is to give thanks for experiences, even the hurtful ones; it is to give thanks for every person, even the hateful ones; it is to see everyone and everything as somehow a part of us; it is to be taught by all.

Sometimes it seems that we choose the hard way of learning. Like the prodigal son, we may seem to be taking the pleasant, easy path, but like him we find ourselves in a far country, feeding on husks, lost and unhappy. How many times has every one of us, like the prodigal son, decided not to stay down or depressed, not to remain in poverty of mind, body, or soul. We too have arisen and gone to God. And out of a sad or bitter time we have found ourselves; we have entered the circle of God's love; we have realized that always we have been one with God, with our good. The unhappiness is behind us; we are stronger, wiser than before; we know now who we are and where we belong.

If all things and all persons are our teachers, why is it that we do not always learn the lesson that is there for us? Why is it that we seem to go through the same experiences again and again?

A person, for instance, may have a most disagreeable and unpleasant neighbor. Nothing seems to help the situation; the neighbor only seems to grow more hateful. So the person moves to get away from the neighbor. In the different locality, with different neighbors, he often finds it to be the same old story. A new neighbor appears on the scene, as hateful as, if not worse than, the one before.

Until we meet a situation from within, learn from it, grow through it, we shall find it facing us again and again—in a different shape and form perhaps, but essentially the same problem.

We do not need to meet the same problems again and again. We have great capacities for spiritual growth within us. The more we are aware of ourselves as spiritual beings, the more we realize that we are one with the Mind of God, the more we shall grow and unfold and come into the possession and use of our full powers.

There are splendid potentialities in us all; we are meant for greatness and goodness. We have a larger work to do than we can envision. Just as true education is not a cramming into the mind of knowledge from without but a drawing forth of the innate wisdom that is within, so our powers are developed as we let go of outer striving and work inwardly.

Prayer is a way of calling into expression all the God-powers and God-potentialities that are within us. True prayer is a lifting of our thoughts and feelings, a lifting of our whole being to God. True prayer is the realization of oneness with God, the realization in which the little self drops away and we stand tall in the divine Presence, we know ourselves as children of light.

It is prayer that quickens our awareness, that inspires us to use Truth in our thinking, that releases the force of love in us and through us.

When we are aware of the powers within us, when we gauge our attitudes and reactions by the Christ standard of love and understanding, of wisdom and forgiveness, we learn and grow every day of our lives. We are not only shaped and molded as before by experiences, but now as possessors of spiritual power we shape and mold our world. We are not at the mercy of conditions. We see the power of God at work, no matter what the appearances; and we call the transforming power into activity through our faith and through our words of Truth.

If we find ourselves in the midst of some situation that seems difficult or hard to bear, if we are having trouble getting along with some person, if for any reason we are troubled or unhappy, let us look at these situations, these persons, these conditions, and say: "You are my teachers. I have something to learn from you." To face life in this way is to find ourselves, to discover that the power of God is with us. We will no longer wish that we were in some place other than where we are now. We will see that we do indeed stand on holy ground.

Chapter 42

God Is With You

God is with you. You need never feel alone, for you are one with God; where you are, God is.

As you go about your day's tasks, God is with you. When you walk along a busy street, God is with you. When you shop, when you visit with friends, when you are by yourself, God is with you.

Right where you are, God is with you. As you read these words, God is there with you, a loving presence and power. You do not have to wait until you stop to pray to feel God near; your every breath proclaims God; in God you live and move and have your being.

Do you need healing? God is with you as life. You are part of the eternal life of God; out of this life you came forth; in and through this life you are sustained. When you think about your body, think of it as being the temple of the living God; think of it as filled with the life of God; think of this life as flowing freely through you.

To realize that God is with you is to realize healing; for where God is there is life, where God is there is healing power. The life you seek, the healing you pray for is already yours, for God is with you as life.

In meeting your responsibilities, in making decisions, large and small, in handling your everyday concerns, do you ever long for more wisdom and understanding? Wisdom, guidance, a sense of rightness and direction can be yours as you realize that God is with you as wisdom, as understanding, as insight. Spirit in you is all-wise, all-knowing. Whatever you turn over to the Holy Spirit in you is made clear.

God is with you as light. This light shines into your mind and illumines you; this light brightens your thoughts, this light makes all things plain. Whenever you feel in the dark about anything, declare that God is with you as wisdom and light. The answer you have been seeking will come. You will find it easy to meet your responsibilities, to make decisions, to meet all the issues of life effectively.

God is with you as power. You do not create power. The power is there, within you. All you have to do is let this power come forth. You may feel inadequate to the demands made upon you, but the Truth is that you have the power of God in you. When you affirm God's power, when you rely on it, you find that you are able to accomplish things you had thought impossible. With God all things are possible, and God is with you; God's power works in and through you.

God is with you, and because God is with you, you need never feel weak or helpless. God is strength; God is your strength. God is your strength of mind and body, the strength that sustains and supports you, that carries you through difficult times or conditions. God is the strength of your heart, the strength of your emotions. It may seem that something cannot be borne, but through God there is always the strength you need.

The strength of God is a joyous strength. When you abide in the faith that God is with you, that God's strength is with you, you are filled with joy.

Do you ever have times when you feel unloved, unwanted? Do not ever let yourself believe that this is true, for you are loved with an everlasting love. God loves you. God needs you. This is what you are to remember always; this is the secret that you must keep in your heart and act upon in your thinking and living.

You feel differently, you think differently, you act differently when you have the inner conviction that God loves you, that you are God's child, that your life has meaning and purpose in God. Instead of longing for other people to love you, instead of longing for things or circumstances to bring you happiness, you are so filled with the love of God that you express it to all and attract it from all. You are so filled with the love of God that happiness is your continual inner state, a happiness that is not dependent on things or outer circumstances. God is with you, and because God is with you, love is with you. The longing you may have sometimes for more love in your life is God within you saying to you, "Express Me, express My love."

God is with you. Wherever you are, whatever your need, God is with you as the perfect answer.

You are right now in the presence of God, and in this presence is perfect good. God is with you as life; God is with you as wisdom; God is with you as power; God is with you as strength; God is with you as love. God is with you as your all-in-all.

About the Author

Martha Smock's involvement in Unity School of Christianity, the nondenominational, international, metaphysical movement, began at an early age. Born in Kansas City, Missouri, in 1913, she grew up in Unity, attending Sunday school from age two. Her mother was a close friend of Unity's co-founders, Charles and Myrtle Fillmore. In her late teens, Martha joined the staff of Unity School as a letter writer in Silent Unity, the international prayer ministry. Subsequently, she became an instructor in the Letter Writing Department and in 1944 was named editor of *Daily Word*, Unity's most popular magazine.

Martha Smock remained editor of *Daily Word* for over thirty years. She described it as a magazine of today: "*Daily Word* is what it was intended to be in the beginning. It serves as a daily reminder that nothing is hopeless or impossible and reaffirms that we are spiritual beings who can meet any situation happily, effectively, and constructively."

Martha also wrote three books in addition to this one, *Halfway Up the Mountain, Turning Points,* and *Listen, Beloved.* She spoke at retreats and conferences at Unity's headquarters in Unity Village, Missouri, and was a guest speaker at ministries throughout the United States. In 1980, Martha was ordained a Unity minister.

Martha and her husband Carl raised two daughters, Stephanie and Kathy, and lived in Mission Hills, Kansas.

Listed in *Who's Who in American Women* since 1974,

Martha brought people from all walks of life to a closer understanding of the practical application of Christian principles in daily living. Reverend Smock made her transition in 1984.

Printed U.S.A.   77-6539-75C-12-94